ON CRIMES AND
PUNISHMENTS

CESARE BECCARIA

ON CRIMES AND PUNISHMENTS

Translated from the Italian
in the Author's Original Order

With Notes and Introduction by
David Young

HACKETT PUBLISHING COMPANY

Cesare Beccaria: 1738–1794
On Crimes and Punishments was first published in 1764

Cover design by Listenberger Associates
Book design by J. M. Matthew

First edition
19 18 17 16 15 14   6 7 8 9 10 11

For further information, please address
    Hackett Publishing Company, Inc.
    P. O. Box 44937
    Indianapolis, Indiana 46244-0937

    www.hackettpublishing.com

Library of Congress Cataloging-in-Publication Data

Beccaria, Cesare, marchese di, 1738–1794.
    On crimes and punishments.
    Translation of: Dei delitti e delle pene.
    Bibliography: p.
    Includes index.
    1. Punishment—Europe—Early works to 1800.
2. Criminal justice, Administration of—Europe—
Early works to 1800.   3. Beccaria, Cesare, marchese di,
1738–1794. 4. Lawyers—Italy—Biography. I. Title.
HV8661.B26 1986   364.6   85-17578
ISBN 0-915144-99-9
ISBN 0-915145-97-9 (pbk.)

ISBN-13: 978-0-915144-99-0 (cloth)
ISBN-13: 978-0-915145-97-3 (pbk.)

To
Flossie, Michael, Jay, and Spencer

Contents

| XLV. | Education | 79 |

| XLVI. | Of Pardons | 80 |

| XLVII. | Conclusion | 81 |

| | *Notes* | *83* |

Acknowledgments

I am grateful to Dr. Robert Shackleton of All Souls College, Oxford, under whose guidance I first studied Beccaria. I am likewise grateful to the National Endowment for the Humanities, which granted me a stipend to participate in a postdoctoral summer seminar on the philosophy of crime and punishment. Professor Jeffrie Murphy, the director of that seminar, deepened my understanding, read portions of the manuscript of the translation, and made many valuable suggestions. My colleagues in the seminar also offered many useful ideas. I thank Professors Lando Landi and Gianni Francioni of the University of Pavia for providing me with valuable materials and stimulating ideas. I am grateful to those who read the manuscript on behalf of Hackett Publishing and for their much-needed advice. Mary Lee Sabastian did an excellent work in preparing the manuscript. Any faults in this edition are my own.

DAVID YOUNG

Introduction

Cesare Beccaria (1738–1794) is known almost exclusively as the author of *On Crimes and Punishments,* a short book on criminal law reform that excited keen interest and great controversy when it was first published in 1764 and that still commands attention both for some of the issues it raises and for the answers it suggests. In many respects, however, the book was greater than its self-effacing author, a man of almost crippling shyness. Neither before nor after the publication of his seminal work did he do much to distinguish himself beyond the confines of Lombardy, his native province.

The eldest son of an aristocratic Milanese family, Beccaria received an education which he later described as "fanatical," studying at the Jesuit school in Parma and taking his law degree at the University of Pavia in 1758. In 1761, he fell madly in love with a young woman of lesser social standing than his own, and he eventually married her despite the vehement protests of his father, who claimed the full authority of a patrician *paterfamilias.*

At about the time of these domestic quarrels, Beccaria met and came under the influence of Pietro Verri, another Milanese aristocrat ten years Beccaria's senior. Verri had traveled abroad and had become familiar with the writings of British economists and French *philosophes.* Eager to bring Italy into the mainstream of Enlightenment culture and to institute practical reforms in Lombardy, which was under Austrian rule, Verri was at the center of a group of young men known as the "Academy of Fists." It was in the Verri circle that Beccaria began to read Enlightenment authors, and it was at the suggestions of Pietro Verri that Beccaria undertook to write a brief work on criminal justice. Although busy with their own projects, other members of the Academy of Fists aided Beccaria, and the first copies of *On Crimes and Punishments* were printed in the summer of 1764.

The book was an immediate sensation. In large measure, this was because Beccaria went beyond the narrow confines of criminal law (he knew relatively little about the technicalities of criminal justice) and placed his subject in a broad social and philosophic context. Criminal law is designed to uphold certain values and to support a certain type of society, and, implicitly or explicitly, Beccaria was calling for very broad changes when he argued for drastic alterations in methods of dealing with crime. In his own day and since, many of Beccaria's admirers have seen his book as the protest of evident justice and humanity against an archaic, cruel, and repressive system. Other readers, less sympathetic, have seen in Beccaria's work a pleading for "bourgeois" interests, "despotic" state power, and efficient rather than humane justice.

The criminal justice systems of Europe in the eighteenth century were open to criticism on a number of counts. There was often cruelty in the investigation and punishment of crime. Judicial torture was frequently used, and the death penalty was common even for relatively minor crimes. Almost everywhere, the law reflected the common assumption that political loyalty and good behavior were best secured by religious uniformity. Reliance on tradition and ancient custom tended to reinforce the powers of local courts and parochial elites—the "intermediate powers" that Montesquieu had praised—and to circumscribe the central authority of the state. In most countries, equality before the law was not recognized, even in principle; different rules applied to different levels of the social hierarchy. The law's vagueness, contradictions, and wide scope for interpretation and discretion tended to reinforce the personal dependence of the disadvantaged on those with inherited property and authority. The advantaged could apply, mitigate, or withhold criminal sanctions, whereas the disadvantaged were usually those against whom the laws were enforced.

Beccaria certainly did not accept this criminal justice system or the values upon which it was based. Nonetheless, he was not a radical bent on overthrowing authority or all existing institutions. Instead, he drew on a wide variety of Enlightenment sources to build a series of reform proposals, not just for criminal legislation but for social organization generally. His work combines disparate elements, perhaps not always successfully or harmoniously. On the one hand, he was drawn to the utilitarianism of Helvétius who evaluated all institutions by their capacity for producing the greatest possible social happiness. Bentham would later elaborate such doctrines into a full-blown theory of legislation, acknowledging his debt to Beccaria as he did so. On the other hand, Beccaria seemed equally attracted to the doctrines of natural individual rights propounded by seventeenth-century writers and developed in the eighteenth century by Rousseau. Such thinking emphasized justice and individual autonomy as the proper foundations of society and pointed toward the retributivist, anti-utilitarian theories of Kant and Hegel. Despite these and other tensions in his work, the main outlines of the society that Beccaria wanted are clear enough.

First, although Beccaria was no freethinker, he did want to secularize social institutions in general and criminal law in particular. Ferdinando Facchinei, a monk who lived in Venetian territory and who was Beccaria's earliest and most perceptive conservative critic, rightly noted that *On Crimes and Punishments* treated human happiness in this world as the chief goal of society. Beccaria was eager to distinguish sharply between sin and crime, to deny the political necessity of religious uniformity, and to limit the wealth, authority, and influence of the clergy.

Beccaria, however, did not suppose that individual virtues and social institutions have nothing to do with one another. As Facchinei was quick to see, Beccaria wanted to encourage certain virtues, but ones far different from those supported in most legal codes of the time. Beccaria rejected the military virtues characteristic of a traditional landed aristocracy and the religious virtues of ascetic self-denial. Instead, he sought to encourage the values of a competitive, commercial society: love of economic gain, prudent calculation of self-interest, tolerance for diversity of opinion, and the cultivation of "luxury," or higher standards of living.

In light of this apparent desire for capitalistic economic development, it may seem odd that Beccaria referred to private property as a "terrible and perhaps unnecessary right." Neither in *On Crimes and Punishments* nor in his later lectures on political economy, however, did Beccaria ever seriously advocate abolishing all private property, and the establishment of complete economic equality was certainly not among his goals. There were certain types of property, however, that Beccaria and other members of the Academy of Fists did want to see eliminated. Notable among these were clerical mortmain and entails. By mortmain, property that passed into the hands of the church was bound to remain there forever. By the entailing of estates, a device especially favored by the landed nobility, family property was kept perpetually inalienable, indivisible, and indisputably under the control of the current head of the family. Entails thus preserved the wealth and status of the family from generation to generation. Beccaria and his colleagues attacked both these forms of property as constricting the circulation of wealth and hampering the development of a spirit of enterprise. They argued that neither a magnate with a guaranteed income nor a commoner without hope of

achieving wealth and status would have any incentive to engage in eco-
nomically beneficial activity or innovation. Riches, they maintained,
should circulate freely, and property and prestige should be the reward
of merit and vigorous action, not of birth. Clerical mortmain and aristocratic entails stood in the way of economic progress and equality of
opportunity.

Beccaria's desire for equality of opportunity was closely linked to
another of his major objectives, equality before the law. In a dynamic
society in which wealth and status were, in principle, open to everyone,
the law could not serve to reinforce distinctions and privileges based solely
on birth; indeed, the law could not tolerate them at all. Rather, the law
would have to be an impartial arbiter among theoretically equal com-
petitors, applying equal sanctions to anyone who indulged in antisocial
behavior. Beccaria argued that, as a matter of principle, laws would have
to be considered as "pacts among free men." As a matter of utility, he
contended, less criminal behavior would occur if the law were seen as
emanating equally from all citizens and applying equally to all.

In the sort of society Beccaria wanted, both the law itself and its
enforcement would be impersonal. Hence Beccaria stood as a champion
of enlightened despotism. He declared that only a centralized state headed
by a well-advised monarch had the power to institute a clear, rational
legal code, to break down the powers of local elites, and to build a desirable social organization. Further, as was made clear by the writings of
his colleagues and his own later lectures on political economy, the crown
was seen as the ideal agent for breaking down internal trade barriers and
promoting economic growth. Beccaria's proposals would surely advance
the monarch's power as well as enhance the ruler's revenue. Beccaria's
chief concern, however, was to break down a system that reinforced bonds
of personal dependence and hereditary privilege. He had no desire to
substitute one form of personal authority for another. Thus he was at
pains to argue that the power of the sovereign to grant pardons on an
individual basis should be used with the utmost circumspection, and, ide-
ally, it should be eliminated altogether.

Finally, Beccaria urged that the law should be mild and humane.
Characteristically, he often appealed to arguments of utility and to arguments from natural or human rights. Thus he attacked judicial torture,
both because it was not useful in discovering the true facts of a case and
because it violated the right of the accused to self-defense—or, at least,
his right not to be a party to his own destruction. Thus Beccaria became

the first major writer to call for the abolition of the death penalty. On the one hand, he argued that as the death penalty is an ineffective deterrant, a sentence of a lifetime at hard labor will better serve the utilitarian purpose. On the other, he carried the notion of a natural right to self-preservation, common in many seventeenth-century theories of natural law, to its logical extreme. Beccaria suggested that a right to one's own life is indefeasible, and, even if it were not, interpretative charity should create a strong presumption that no one would ever alienate power over his life to the sovereign. In sum, Beccaria maintained that a mild legal system is both useful, in that it is likely to win widespread approval, and just, in that it is most in accord with basic human rights.

Drawing on a broad variety of sources in Enlightenment thinking and taking a wide social and political view rather than a narrowly legalistic one, Beccaria propounded a liberal theory of criminal justice, often with cogency and imagination, always with conviction. Many who shared his liberalism, both in the eighteenth century and since, have embraced his work and seen it as a model of both utility and humanity. His work was cited—often effectively—from Florence to Philadelphia, and a number of his proposals became standard features of the legal systems of Europe and North America. Of course, Beccaria has certainly not escaped criticism. From Facchinei onward, paternalistic conservatives have attacked Beccaria for seeking to destroy the personal bonds and religious convictions, which, in their view, hold society together. Those more radical than Beccaria have, from the eighteenth century onward, accused him of turning a blind eye to the inequalities that private property inevitably creates. In their view, the abolition of legal privilege is merely a mask for reinforcing the privileges of wealth with criminal sanctions; equality of opportunity is meaningless without a good measure of substantive equality; and sharp class divisions preclude the kind of consensus or social contract on which Beccaria sought to base his proposals. Further, even those who have shared many of Beccaria's liberal premises have not always shared his conclusions. Kant, for instance, argued that Beccaria often let utilitarian considerations stand in the way of considerations of justice. Kant defended the death penalty against Beccaria's attacks on retributivist grounds. Whether readers have agreed or disagreed with the general principles or the specific proposals of *On Crimes and Punishments,* however, the book has always been stimulating, both for the issues it raises and the solutions it suggests.

After the publication of *On Crimes and Punishments,* Beccaria remained for a time a member of the Verri circle, contributing a few articles to *The Coffeehouse,* a moral journal published by Verri and his friends which was modeled on Addison's *Spectator.* In the meantime, the book on criminal justice had attracted international attention, especially among the Parisian Encyclopedists, who rightly recognized many of their own ideas in it. On behalf of the French *philosophes,* the Abbé André Morellet invited Beccaria to Paris. Although devoted to quiet domesticity and terrified at the thought of leaving Milan, Beccaria left in October 1766. Once in Paris, his shy, self-effacing personality failed to meet the expectations raised by his book, and he cut short his stay, returning precipitously to Milan. Pietro Verri was disgusted by what he considered his erstwhile friend's infantile behavior, not least because it seemed to reflect badly on the entire circle of enlightened Lombard reformers. Beccaria's close association with the Verri group thereupon was at an end.

Most of the remainder of Beccaria's life was devoted to practical work in the Austrian bureaucracy. From 1769 to 1771, he held the chair of political economy at the Palatine School of Milan, an institution designed to prepare young men for future government service. His lectures continued a number of the themes first taken up in *On Crimes and Punishments.* Although he was urged to put his notes in order, his course on political economy was not published until after his death. He did publish a treatise on style that was received without enthusiasm. It was his last major intellectual effort. After 1771, Beccaria held a number of civil service positions in Lombardy, contributing to, but scarcely serving as a leader in, the implementation of some of the liberal reforms he had advocated earlier in his career. His death in 1794 went all but unnoticed outside his immediate family. *On Crimes and Punishments,* however, was still considered a landmark work in the field of criminal justice and was still widely discussed. Seeming to rise above its author, the book remains important, both for the points it raises in the area of criminal law and in the broader realm of moral and social considerations that serves as the foundation of criminal justice.

Note on the Text

Establishing "the" text of *On Crimes and Punishments* is scarcely an easy task, and even the authorship of the book has been called into question. Beyond doubt, the work grew out of discussions in the Verri circle, and both Pietro Verri and his younger brother Alessandro provided Beccaria with advice and suggestions. Beccaria prepared a book manuscript based upon these discussions, but, before the work went to the printer, Pietro Verri edited it, altering its arrangement, breaking down long chapters into shorter ones, excising some of Beccaria's material, and adding (or recommending) new material as well. Beccaria accepted these changes and the book was published in 1764. Beccaria made still further changes in later editions. Later, after the rupture between Beccaria and his erstwhile friends, Pietro Verri, certainly by no means a disinterested source, wrote down a number of letters stressing his own role in preparing *On Crimes and Punishments*. Never, however, did the Verri brothers flatly deny Beccaria's authorship, and, although he undoubtedly received a great deal of help, Beccaria was and is still regarded as the one responsible for *On Crimes and Punishments*.

Matters were complicated further when, in 1765, the Abbé André Morellet undertook to translate the book into French. Not only did he translate, however; he took it upon himself to rearrange the work, transposing sentences, paragraphs, and entire sections. The major result was to change Beccaria's book from a rather free essay into a more rigidly logical treatise; another result was to emphasize the utilitarian elements in the book. Even among the other Parisian *philosophes*, Morellet's operation did not meet with complete approval. Melchior Grimm declared that there would have been a general uprising if anyone had tried to rearrange Montesquieu's *The Spirit of the Laws* in this way, even to make it more "logical." The anonymous English translator of the 1769 London edition of *On Crimes and Punishments* stated flatly that Morellet had "assumed a right which belongs not to any translator and which cannot be justified."

Beccaria's own attitude toward Morellet's changes is hard to determine. Beccaria wrote to Morellet in January 1766, ostensibly approving the Frenchman's changes. With this supposed blessing from the author, Morellet's arrangement gradually became standard, not only in French editions of the book but in all languages. On the other hand, Beccaria's letter can be seen as evasive rather than approving. It would have been quite out of character for the timid Milanese to condemn flatly the work of one of the Parisian intellectuals whom he considered his masters, but his subsequent actions certainly demonstrated no endorsement of Morellet's editorial work. Thus, although Beccaria promised that he would incorporate most, if not all, of the Frenchman's alterations into forthcoming Italian editions of the book, he continued to use the previous arrangement in the editions that he personally supervised. Beccaria was willing to put Pietro Verri's alterations into the book but seemed less willing to accept Morellet's.

The text of the present translation, then, is based upon the sixth and final edition that Beccaria personally oversaw, published at Leghorn in 1766 and bearing the false place impression of Haarlem. This was the text chosen by Franco Venturi for his excellent 1965 Italian edition. If it would be going too far to say that this arrangement represents Beccaria's "own" version of the work, it is nevertheless the version that contains the alterations that he was willing to use, and it may be said to be the version that best represents the thinking of the circle of Milanese reformers to which Beccaria belonged.

For readers who wish to pursue textual questions further, the best recent scholarship on the subject is Gianni Francioni, *La prima redazione del "Dei delitti e delle pene"* (Naples, 1981). For a strong argument in favor of preferring the text used here to Morellet's arrangement, see the editorial comments in *Illuministi italiani,* vol. 3, *Riformatori lombardi, piemontesi, e toscani,* ed. Franco Venturi (Milan and Naples, 1958), pp. 23–26. See also the editor's introduction to Cesare Beccaria, *Dei delitti e delle pene. Con una raccolta di lettere e documenti relativi alla nascita dell'opera e alla sua fortuna nell'Europa del Settecento,* ed. Franco Venturi (Turin, 1965), esp. pp. xx–xxi, xxxvii–xxxviii. Beccaria's letter to Morellet is contained in this edition, pp. 361–69.

Further Reading

For those seeking further reading in English, the best place to begin is the biography by Marcello Maestro, *Cesare Beccaria and the Origins of Penal Reform* (Philadelphia, 1973). Maestro's scholarship is meticulous, and he presents a good deal of information about Milan in the eighteenth century and about the international reception of Beccaria's work. Stuart Woolf, *A History of Italy, 1700–1860* (London, 1979), and John W. Roberts, "Enlightened Despotism in Italy," Harold Acton et al., *Art and Ideas in Eighteenth-Century Italy* (Rome, 1960), pp. 25–44, both furnish valuable insights into the historical context of the Italian Enlightenment in general and of Beccaria in particular. For the role of Beccaria and his friends in the political, economic, and intellectual life of Lombardy, both as theoreticians and practical reformers, Daniel M. Klang, "Reform and Enlightenment in Eighteenth-Century Lombardy," *Canadian Journal of History/Annales Canadiennes d'Histoire* 19 (1984): 39–70, is a concise and penetrating overview.

A number of interpreters have been Beccaria as a champion of virtually self-evident principles of justice and humanity. Maestro's biography, mentioned above, presents *On Crimes and Punishments* in such a light, as does Peter Gay, *The Enlightenment: An Interpretation*, vol. 2, *The Science of Freedom*, pp. 423–447. In a sophisticated effort to place the moderation of punishment in the context of broad social development, Jan Gorecki, *Capital Punishment: Criminal Law and Social Evolution* (New York, 1983), takes a substantially similar view of Beccaria. Other critics, however, have argued that Beccaria's work had an underside and that its arguments were tied to rather narrow economic and political interests; see Klang's essay, mentioned above. Drew Humphries and David F. Greenberg, "The Dialectics of Crime Control," in *Crime and Capitalism*, ed. David F. Greenberg (Palo Alto, Cal., 1981), pp. 209–254, present a Marxist perspective on changes in criminology during the eighteenth and nineteenth centuries; they suggest that Beccaria was an aristocratic spokesman for a bourgeois ideology. In a controversial work, Michel Foucault, *Discipline and Punish: The Birth of the Prison*, trans. Alan Sheridan (New York, 1977), maintains that the movement for criminal law reform of which Beccaria was a part arose from an impulse toward greater social control rather than a higher degree of justice or humanity. Philip Jenkins, "Varieties of Enlightenment Criminology," *The British Journal of Criminology* 24 (1984): 112–30, contends that Beccaria played a basically conservative role, using Englightenment ideas in such a way as to uphold authority, property, and the responsibility of individual criminals for their own acts, while turning aside the potentially unsettling streams of relativism, scientific determinism, and social radicalism in eighteenth-century thought.

ON CRIMES AND PUNISHMENTS

In rebus quibuscumque difficilioribus non expectandum, ut quis simul, et serut, et metat, sed praeparatione opus est, ut per gradus maturescant.

Francis Bacon, *Sermones fideles*, n. XLVII

"In all negociations of difficulty, a man may not look to sow and reap at once; but must prepare business, and so ripen it by degrees."
Bacon, "Of Negociating," *Essays*, XLVII

TO THE READER[1]

Some remains of the laws of an ancient conquering people, compiled on the authority of a prince who reigned twelve centuries ago in Constantinople,[2] later mingled with Lombard customs[3] and collected in hodge-podge volumes by unofficial and obscure commentators—this is what forms the traditional opinions that in a large part of Europe are nonetheless called "law." Moreover, it is today as pernicious as it is common that an opinion of Carpzov, an ancient custom cited by Claro, or a torture suggested with irate complacency by Farinacci should be the laws unhesitatingly followed by those who ought to dispose of the lives and fortunes of men only with diffidence.[4] These laws, which are an emanation of the most barbarous ages, are examined in this book to the extent that they concern the criminal system. In a style that will have no appeal to the unenlightened and impatient mob, we are taking the liberty of exposing their confusion to those charged with the public welfare. The sincere search for truth and the independence from accepted opinion with which this work is written are the result of the mild and enlightened government under which the author lives.[5] The great monarchs and benefactors of humanity who rule here love the truths that an obscure philosopher expounds, not with fanaticism, but with a zeal aroused only by those who, rejecting reason, have recourse to violence or fraud. Current disorders, as anyone who examines all the circumstances well will see, mock and reproach previous ages, not this one or its legislators.

Whoever would wish to honor me with his criticisms, then, should begin with a sound understanding of the goal toward which this work is directed, a goal which, far from diminishing legitimate authority, should serve to increase it, if ideas carry more weight with men than force and if that authority is justified in everyone's eyes by its mildness and humanity. The ill-intentioned criticisms published against this book[6] are founded on confused notions and oblige me to interrupt my arguments to enlightened readers for a moment in order to bar the door once and for all against errors arising from timid zeal or calumnies arising from malign envy.

There are three sources from which the moral and political principles that regulate men are derived: revelation, natural law, and the artificial conventions of society. There can be no comparison between the first and the other two as far as its main purpose is concerned, but all three are at one in

1

that they all lead to happiness in this mortal life. The consideration of the relationships resulting from the last of these sources in no way excludes those that
result from the first two, but revelation and natural law, though divine and immutable, have been changed by human fault in a thousand ways, by false
religions and by arbitrary notions of vice and virtue in depraved minds. Aside
from any other consideration, then, it seems necessary to examine the effects
of purely human conventions, which are expressly formulated or simply
assumed in view of common necessity and utility. The idea of common
necessity and utility is one on which every sect and every moral system must
necessarily agree,[7] and it will always be a praiseworthy undertaking to compel
even the most stubborn and incredulous people to conduct themselves according to the principles that induce men to live in society. Thus, there are three
distinct classes of virtue and vice: religious, natural, and political. These three
classes should never be in contradiction with one another, but not all the
duties and consequences that derive from one derive from the others. Not
everything that religion requires is required by natural law, nor is all that
natural law requires demanded by purely social law. It is, however, most important to set apart the results of this last-named convention, that is, of the express or tacit pacts among men, because such is the limit of the force that may
be used legitimately between one man and another without a special commis-
sion from the Supreme Being. Thus, the idea of political virtue may, quite
legitimately, be deemed variable; the concept of natural virtue would always
be clear and obvious if the stupidity or the passions of men did not obscure it;
the idea of religious virtue is always one and the same because it is revealed
directly by God and is maintained by Him.

It would be an error, then, to attribute to someone who speaks of social
conventions and their consequences principles contrary to natural law or to
revelation, for he is not talking about them. It would be an error for someone
speaking of the state of war before the establishment of society to take this in
the sense that Hobbes did, that is, as a state without previously established
obligations, instead of considering this struggle as something born of the cor-
ruption of human nature and the absence of any express sanction.[8] It would be
an error to blame a writer who is examining the effects of the social contract
for not admitting those effects before the existence of the contract itself.

Divine and natural justice are by their essence immutable and constant, since the relationship between two similar objects is always the same. On
the other hand, human, or rather political, justice, since it is only a relationship between action and the variable condition of society, may itself vary to
the degree that the action in question becomes useful or necessary to society,

and one can form a clear idea of this only by an analysis of the infinitely complicated relationships and mutations of social arrangements. As soon as these
essentially distinct principles become confused with one another, there can be
no hope of reasoning well in political matters. It is the task of theologians to
establish the limits of justice and injustice regarding the intrinsic goodness or
wickedness of an act; it is the task of the observer of public life to establish the
relationships of political justice and injustice, that is, of what is useful or harmful to society. Moreover, one of these goals cannot by prejudicial to the other,
for everyone realizes how much political virtue must yield to the immutable
virtue that comes from God.

Whoever would wish to honor me with his criticisms, I repeat, should
not begin, then, by supposing that I hold principles which are subversive
either of virtue or of religion, for I have shown that such are not my principles;
and, instead of making me out to be irreligious or seditious, let him try to find
me a bad logician or an unwary and naive commentator on political matters.
Let him not tremble at every proposition that supports the interests of
humanity; let him convince me of the uselessness of my principles or of the
political damage that would result from them, and let him show me the advantages of established practices. I have given public testimony of my religion
and of my obedience to my sovereign in the reply to the *Notes and Observa-
tions*,[9] it would be superfluous to answer other writings of this sort. But anyone
who will write with the decency that becomes honorable men and with enough
intelligence to free me from proving elementary principles, of whatever
character he may be, will find me not so much a man eager to reply in his own
defense as a peaceful friend of truth.*

---

*All the passages enclosed by this sign: / are the first additions, and those enclosed
by this sign: // are the second additions.[10]

INTRODUCTION

Generally speaking, men leave the most important regulations to day-to-day prudence or to the discretion of those whose interest it is to oppose the most provident laws. The nature of such laws is to make life's benefits universal and to resist the force that causes these advantages to become concentrated in a few hands, placing on one side the extremity of power and happiness and, on the other, all weakness and misery. Thus, only after having passed through a thousand errors in matters most essential to life and liberty and after having grown weary of suffering evils that strain the limits of endurance are men induced to remedy the disorders which oppress them. Then they recognize the most evident truths; these, by their very simplicity, escape uneducated minds, which are not accustomed to analysis and which receive ready-made impressions from tradition rather than through examination.

Let us open our history books, and we shall see that laws, which are or ought to be agreements among free men, usually have been the instrument of the passions of a few persons. Sometimes laws arise from a fortuitous and transient necessity, but they have never been dictated by an impartial observer of human nature who can grasp the actions of a multitude of men and consider them from this point of view: *the greatest happiness shared among the greatest number.*[1] Happy are those very few nations that have not waited for the slow movement of happenstance and human vicissitudes to make excessive evil give way to progress toward goodness but that have accelerated the intermediate stages with good laws! Further, mankind owes a debt of gratitude to the philosopher who, from the despised obscurity of his study, had the courage to cast the first and long fruitless seeds of useful truths among the multitude!

We now know the proper relationships between subject and sovereign and among different nations; commerce has been quickened by the appearance of philosophic truths spread by the printing press, and a quiet war of industry has broken out among nations, the most humane sort of war and the kind most worthy of reasonable men.[2] These are the fruits that we owe to the enlightenment of this century. Very few people, however, have examined and fought against the cruelty of punishments and the irregularity of criminal procedure, a part of legislation that is so fundamental and so neglected almost everywhere in Europe. Very few people, by going back to general principles,

5

have destroyed the errors accumulated over several centuries, or at least used the strength of recognized truth to check the unbridled course of ill-directed power, which, up to now, has set a long and supposedly authoritative example of cold-blooded atrocity. And yet the trembling of the weak, sacrificed to cruel ignorance and wealthy indolence; the barbarous and useless tortures multiplied with prodigal and useless severity for crimes that are either unproven or chimerical; the squalor and horrors of a prison, augmented by uncertainty, that most cruel tormentor of the wretched—these should have aroused the attention of the kind of magistrates who guide the opinions of human minds.

The immortal President de Montesquieu touched hastily on this matter. Indivisible truth has compelled me to follow the shining footsteps of this great man. The thinking men for whom I write, however, will know how to tell my trail from his.[3] I shall count myself fortunate if I, as did he, can earn the secret gratitude of the little-known and peace-loving followers of reason and if I can inspire that sweet thrill with which sensitive souls respond to whoever upholds the interests of humanity!

I

ORIGIN OF PUNISHMENTS

Laws are the conditions by which independent and isolated men, tired of living in a constant state of war and of enjoying a freedom made useless by the uncertainty of keeping it, unite in society.[1] They sacrifice a portion of this liberty in order to enjoy the remainder in security and tranquillity. The sum of all these portions of liberty sacrificed for the good of everyone constitutes the sovereignty of a nation, and the sovereign is its legitimate depository and administrator. The mere formation of this deposit, however, was not sufficient; it had to be defended against the private usurpations of each particular individual, for everyone always seeks to withdraw not only his own share of liberty from the common store, but to expropriate the portions of other men besides. Tangible motives were required sufficient to dissuade the despotic spirit of each man from plunging the laws of society back into the original chaos. These tangible motives are the punishments established for lawbreakers. I say "tangible motives," since experience has shown that the common crowd does not adopt stable principles of conduct, and the universal principle of dissolution which we see in the physical and the moral world cannot be avoided except by motives that have a direct impact on the senses and appear continually to the mind to counterbalance the strong impressions of individual passions opposed to the general good. Neither eloquence nor declamations nor even the most sublime truths have sufficed for long to check the emotions aroused by the vivid impressions of immediately present objects.[2]

II

THE RIGHT
TO PUNISH

Every punishment which does not derive from absolute necessity, says the great Montesquieu, is tyrannical.[1] The proposition may be made general thus: every act of authority between one man and another that does not derive from absolute necessity is tyrannical. Here, then, is the foundation of the sovereign's right to punish crimes: the necessity of defending the depository of the public welfare against the usurpations of private individuals. Further, the more just punishments are, the more sacred and inviolable is personal security, and the greater is the liberty that the sovereign preserves for his subjects. Let us consult the human heart, and there we shall find the fundamental principles of the sovereign's right to punish crimes, for no lasting advantage is to be expected from political morality if it is not founded upon man's immutable sentiments. Any law that deviates from them will always encounter a resistance that will overpower it sooner or later, just as a continually applied force, however slight, eventually overcomes any violent movement communicated to a physical body.

No man freely gave up a part of his own liberty for the sake of the public good; such an illusion exists only in romances. If it were possible, each of us would wish that the agreements binding on others were not binding on himself. Every man thinks of himself as the center of all the world's affairs.

/The increase in the numbers of mankind, slight in itself but too much for the means that sterile and uncultivated nature offered to satisfy increasingly interrelated needs, led the first savages to unite. These initial groups necessarily created others to resist the former, and thus the state of war was transposed from individuals to nations.[2]/

It was necessity, then, that constrained men to give up part of their personal liberty; hence, it is certain that each man wanted to put only the least possible portion into the public deposit, only as much as necessary to induce others to defend it.[3] The aggregate of these smallest possible portions of individual liberty constitutes the right to punish; everything beyond that is an abuse and not justice, a fact but scarcely a right. Note that the word "right" is not a contradiction of the word "force"; the former is, rather, a modification of the latter—namely, the modification most useful to the greatest number. By "justice," moreover, I do not mean anything but the bond necessary to hold private interests together. Without it, they would dissolve into the earlier state of incompatibility. All punishments that exceed what is necessary to preserve this bond are unjust by their very nature. One must beware of attaching the idea of something real to this word "justice," as though it were a physical force or a being that actually exists. It is simply a human manner of conceiving things, a manner that has an infinite influence on the happiness of everybody.[4] Most certainly I am not speaking of the other sort of justice that comes from God and that is directly related to the rewards and punishments of the life to come.

III

CONSEQUENCES

The first consequence of these principles is that only the law may decree punishments for crimes, and this authority can rest only with the legislator, who represents all of society united by a social contract.[1] No magistrate (who is a part of society) can justly inflict a punishment on a member of the same society, for a penalty that exceeds the limit fixed by law is the just punishment and another besides. Thus, no magistrate may, on whatever pretext of zeal or the public good, increase the established punishment for a delinquent citizen.

The second consequence is that if every individual member is bound to society, society is likewise bound to every individual member by a contract that, by its very nature, places both parties under obligation./This obligation, which reaches from the throne to the hovel and which is equally binding on the greatest and the most wretched of men, means nothing other than that it is in everybody's interest that the contracts useful to the greatest number should

be observed. Their violation, even by one person, opens the door to anarchy.*/
The sovereign, who represents society itself, can only establish general laws
that apply to all of its members; he cannot, however, pass judgment as to
whether one of them has violated the social contract, for then the nation would
be divided into two parties: one, represented by the sovereign, which alleges
the violation of the contract, and the other, the party of the accused, which
denies it. Hence it is necessary that a third party judge the facts of the case.
This is the reason that there must be a magistrate whose sentences are beyond
appeal and consist of the simple assertion or denial of particular facts.[2]

The third consequence is that if extremely cruel punishments are
useless, even though they were not directly opposed to the public good and to
the very goal of preventing crimes, then such cruelty would nevertheless be
contrary to those beneficent virtues that flow from enlightened reason, which
prefers to command happy men rather than a herd of slaves who constantly
exchange timid cruelties with one another; excessively severe punishments
would also be contrary to justice and to the nature of the social contract itself.

IV

INTERPRETATION
OF THE LAW[1]

There is a fourth consequence: the authority to interpret penal law can
scarcely rest with criminal judges for the good reason that they are not
lawmakers. Judges have not received laws from our forefathers as a family
tradition or a legacy which leaves to posterity only the task of obeying; they
receive them, rather, from a living society or from the sovereign who

/*The word "obligation" is one of the words more frequently used in morals than
in any other discipline; it is an abbreviated symbol for a chain of arguments and
not for an idea. Look for an idea that corresponds to the word "obligation," and
you will not find it; reason about the matter, and you will understand and be
understood./

represents it and who is the depository of the current will of all citizens. Judges do not receive laws as obligations arising from an ancient oath. Such an oath would be void, for the wills currently bound did not exist when the oath was sworn, and it would be unjust, for it would reduce men from a social condition to the condition of a herd. On the contrary, judges receive laws as the result of a tacit or express oath that the united wills of living subjects have sworn to the sovereign, as bonds necessary to restrain and rule the internal ferment of private interests. This is the solid and true authority of the laws. Who, then, will be the legitimate interpreter of the laws? Will it be the sovereign, in other words, the depository of the actual wills of all the people, or will it be the judge, whose only charge is merely to examine whether or not a certain man has committed an action contrary to the laws?

In every criminal case, the judge should come to a perfect syllogism: the major premise should be the general law; the minor premise, the act which does or does not conform to the law; and the conclusion, acquittal or condemnation. If the judge were constrained to form even two syllogisms, or if he were to choose to do so, then the door to uncertainty would be opened.

Nothing is more dangerous than the common axiom that one must consult the spirit of the law. This is a dike that is readily breached by the torrent of opinion. This truth, though it appears a paradox to uneducated minds that are struck more by a trifling contemporary disorder than by the harmful but remote consequences that follow from a false principle rooted in a nation, appears to me to be well established. Our perceptions and all our ideas are linked together; the more complicated they are, the more numerous are the routes that lead to and from them. Everybody has his own point of view, and everybody has a different one at different times. The spirit of the law, then, would be dependent on the good and bad logic of a judge, on a sound or unhealthy digestion, on the violence of his passions, on the infirmities he suffers, on his relations with the victim, and on all the slight forces that change the appearance of every object in the fickle human mind. Thus we see the fate of a citizen change several times in going from one court to another, and we see that the lives of poor wretches are at the mercy of false reasonings or the momentary churning of a judge's humors. The judge deems all this confused series of notions which affect his mind to be a legitimate interpretation. Thus we see the same court punish the same crime in different ways at different times because it consulted the erroneous instability of interpretations rather than the firm and constant voice of the law.

Any confusion arising from the rigorous observation of the letter of the law cannot be compared with the disorders that spring from interpretation.

Such a temporary inconvenience is a motive for making the simple and necessary correction in the words of the law which give rise to any uncertainty, but it puts a stop to the fatal license of arguing, which is the cause of arbitrary and venal controversies. When a fixed legal code that must be observed to the letter leaves the judge no other task than to examine a citizen's actions and to determine whether or not they conform to the written law, when the standard of justice and injustice that must guide the actions of the ignorant as well as the philosophic citizen is not a matter of controversy but of fact, then subjects are not exposed to the petty tyrannies of many men. Such tyrannies are all the more cruel when there is a smaller distance between the oppresser and the oppressed. They are more ruinous than the tyranny of one person, for the despotism of many can be remedied only by the despotism of a single man, and the cruelty of a despot is not proportional to his strength, but to the obstacles he encounters.[2] With fixed and immutable laws, then, citizens acquire personal security. This is just because it is the goal of society, and it is useful because it enables them to calculate precisely the ill consequences of a misdeed. It is just as true that they will acquire a spirit of independence, but this will not be to shake off the laws and resist the supreme magistrates; rather, they will resist those who have dared to claim the sacred name of virtue for their weakness in yielding to their private interests or capricious opinions. These principles will displease those who have assumed the right to pass on to their inferiors the tyrannical blows that they have received from their superiors. I should have everything to fear if the spirit of tyranny went hand-in-hand with a taste for reading.

V

OBSCURITY OF LAWS

If the interpretation of laws is an evil, their obscurity, which necessarily entails interpretation, is obviously another evil, one that will be all the greater if the laws are written in a language that is foreign to the common people. This places them at the mercy of a handful of men, for they cannot judge for themselves the prospect of their own liberty or that of others. A language of this sort transforms a solemn official book into one that is virtually private and domestic. What must we think of mankind when we consider that such is the ingrained custom of a good part of cultured and enlightened Europe![1] The greater the number of people who understand the sacred law code and who have it in their hands, the less frequent crimes will be, for there is no doubt that ignorance and uncertainty concerning punishments aid the eloquence of the passions.

One consequence of these last thoughts is that, without written texts, society will never assume a fixed form of government in which power derives from the whole rather than the parts and in which the laws, which cannot be altered save by the general will, are not corrupted as they move through the crush of private interests. Experience and reason have shown us that the probability and certainty of human traditions decline the farther removed they are from their source. If there is no lasting memorial of the social contract, how will the laws resist the inevitable force of time and the passions?

From this we see how useful the printing press is. It makes the entire public, not just a few people, the depository of the sacred laws.[2] To a great extent, it has dissipated that dark spirit of cabal and intrigue that vanishes when confronted with enlightenment and learning, which its adherents affect to despise and which they really fear. This is the reason that we see the atrocity of crimes diminishing in Europe; this atrocity made our forefathers tremble and become tyrants and slaves by turns. Anyone who is acquainted with the history of the last two or three centuries, and of our own century, will be able to see how the sweetest virtues—humanity, benevolence, tolerance of human errors —sprang from the lap of luxury and easy living.[3] He will see the effects of what is erroneously called ancient simplicity and good faith: humanity cowering under implacable superstition, the avarice and ambition of a few men staining coffers of gold and royal thrones with human blood, private treasons, public massacres, every nobleman a tyrant to the common people, and ministers of the Gospels' truth soiling with blood the hands that touched the God of mercy every day. These things are not the work of this enlightened century, which some people call corrupt.[4]

VI

PROPORTION BETWEEN
CRIMES AND PUNISHMENTS

Not merely is it in the common interest that crimes not be committed, but that they be more infrequent in proportion to the harm they cause society. Therefore, the obstacles that restrain men from committing crimes should be stronger according to the degree that such misdeeds are contrary to the public good and according to the motives which lead people to crimes.[1] Thus, there must be a proportion between crimes and punishments.

It is impossible to prevent all disorders in the universal strife of human passions. They increase at the compound rate of population growth and the intertwining of private interests, which cannot be directed toward the public welfare with geometric precision. In political arithmetic, one must substitute the calculation of probability for mathematical exactitude. //If one glances at history, one will see disorders growing with the boundaries of empires and national sentiment weakening in the same proportion; the inclination to crime grows in proportion to the advantage that each person finds in the disorders themselves.[2] This is the reason why the need to make punishments more severe always increases.//

That gravity-like force that impells us to seek our own well-being can be restrained only to the degree that obstacles are established in opposition to it. The effects of this force are the confused series of human actions. If these clash with one another and damage each other, punishments, which I shall call "political obstacles," forestall their adverse consequences without destroying their impelling cause, which is the very sensibility inherent in man. The legislator acts like the good architect, whose role is to oppose the ruinous course of gravity and to bring to bear everything that contributes to the strength of his building.[3]

Given the necessity of men uniting together, and given the compacts which necessarily result from the very clash of private interests, one may discern a scale of misdeeds wherein the highest degree consists of acts that are directly destructive of society and the lowest of the least possible injustice against one of its individual members. Between these extremes lie all actions

14

contrary to the public good, which are called crimes, and they diminish imperceptibly from the highest to the lowest. If geometry were adaptable to the infinite and obscure arrangements of human activity, there ought to be a corresponding scale of punishments, descending from the most rigorous to the slightest. The wise lawmaker, however, will rest content with noting the chief points and respecting their order, taking care not to decree the highest degree of punishment for the lowest degree of crime. If there were an exact and universal scale of punishments and crimes, we should have an acceptable and general way to measure the degrees of tyranny and liberty, of the stock of humanity or wickedness, in various nations.

Any action whatsoever that does not fall within the two limits mentioned above cannot be called a "crime," and it cannot be punished as such, except by those who have an interest in giving it that name. Among nations, uncertainty regarding these limits has produced a morality that is in conflict with their legislation; laws on the books, moreover, that are mutually exclusive; and a host of laws that expose the most well-behaved people to the most stringent punishments. Hence "vice" and "virtue" have become vague and fluctuating terms, and hence one becomes uncertain about the security of one's own existence; this produces apathy and a fatal slumber in political bodies. Anyone who will read the law codes and the annals of nations with a philosophical eye will almost always find the terms "vice" and "virtue," "good citizen" and "criminal," changing their meaning in the course of centuries, not because of the changing circumstances that befall the country (and thus always in accordance with the common interest), but because of the errors and passions that have successively dominated various legislators. Quite often, one will see that the passions of one century are the foundation of the morality of future centuries, and that the strong passions born of fanaticism and zeal are weakened and gnawed, if I may put it so, by time (which brings all moral and physical phenomena into equilibrium) until they gradually become the conventional wisdom and a useful tool in the hands of the strong and the shrewd. In this manner, the extremely murky notions of honor and virtue are born. They are so murky because they change with time, which makes names outlive the things for which they stand, and because they change with rivers and mountains, which often mark the boundaries not only of physical but of moral geography.

If pleasure and pain are the motives for action among sentient beings, if the invisible Legislator has established reward and punishment among the motives that impel men even to the most sublime actions,[4] then from the inexact distribution of these motives there will arise this contradiction, which is as little noticed as it is quite common: punishments punish the crimes that they themselves have caused. If an equal punishment is meted out to two crimes that offend society unequally, then men find no stronger obstacle standing in the way of committing the more serious crime if it holds a greater advantage for them.[5]

VII

ERRORS IN THE

MEASUREMENT OF PUNISHMENTS

The preceding reflections give me the right to assert that the only true measurement of crimes is the harm done to the nation, and hence those who believe that the intention of the perpetrator is the true measurement of crimes are in error. Intention depends on the actual impression objects make on the mind and on the mind's prior dispositions; these vary in each and every man with the extremely rapid succession of ideas, emotions, and circumstances. Thus, it would be necessary to frame not only a separate law code for each citizen, but a new law for each crime. Sometimes men with the best intention inflict the worst evil on society, and, at other times, they do the greatest good for it with the most wicked will.[1]

Others measure crimes by the dignity of the injured party rather than by the importance of the crime as far as the public good is concerned. If this were the true measurement of crimes, an irreverence against the Being of beings ought to be punished more severely than the assassination of a monarch, the superiority of divine nature counting for infinitely more than the difference in the offense.

Finally, some think that the gravity of sin should play a part in the measurement of crimes.[2] The fallacy of this opinion will be immediately apparent to anyone who impartially examines the correct relationships between men and men and between men and God. The former are relationships of equality. Necessity alone has brought forth from the conflict of passions and the opposition of interests the idea of *common utility*, which is the basis of human justice. The latter are relationships of dependence upon a perfect Being and Creator Who has reserved to Himself alone the right to be legislator and judge at the same time, for only He can be both without adverse consequences. If He has established eternal punishments for anyone who disobeys His omnipotence, what insect will dare to supplement divine justice? What insect will wish to avenge the Being Who is sufficient unto Himself, Who cannot receive impressions of pleasure and pain from objects, and Who alone among all beings acts without being acted upon? The seriousness of sin depends upon the unfathomable malice of the human heart, and finite beings cannot know this without revelation. How, then, can a standard for punishing crimes be drawn from this? In such a case, men might punish when God forgives and forgive when God punishes. If men can be in conflict with the Almighty by offending Him, they can also be so by punishing.[3]

VIII

DIVISION OF CRIMES[1]

We have seen what the true measure of crimes is—namely, *the harm done to society*.[2] This is one of those palpable truths which one needs neither quadrants nor telescopes to discover and which are within the reach of every ordinary intellect. Through a remarkable combination of circumstances, however, such truths have been recognized with decisive certainty only by a handful of thinking men in every nation and every age. But Asiatic notions, passions bedecked with power and authority, have dissipated the simple ideas that probably formed the first philosophy of newborn societies, usually by imperceptible nudges, but sometimes by violent impressions on timid human credulity. The enlightenment of this century seems to be leading us back to these simple ideas, though with a greater firmness obtainable from a mathematically rigorous investigation, a thousand unhappy experiences, and the obstacles themselves. At this point, the proper order of presentation would lead us to distinguish all the different sorts of crimes and the way to punish them, but their changing nature in the different circumstances of various times and places would make this an immensely and tediously detailed task for us. I shall be content to call attention to the most general principles and the most pernicious and widespread errors in order to disabuse both those who, from a poorly understood love of liberty, would desire to establish anarchy and those who would like to reduce men to a cloister-like regularity.

Some crimes are immediately destructive of society or of the person who represents it; some offend against the personal security of a citizen in his life, his goods, or his honor; certain others are actions contrary to what the laws oblige everyone to do or not to do for the sake of the public good. The first, which are the greatest crimes because they do the most harm, are called lese majesty or high treason. Only tyranny and ignorance, which confound the clearest words and ideas, can assign this name (and consequently the ultimate punishment) to crimes of a different nature, thus making men, as on a thousand other occasions, the victims of a word. Every crime, however private it may be, offends society, but not every crime threatens it directly with destruction. Moral actions, like physical ones, have their limited sphere of activity and are circumscribed, like all natural movements, by time and space. Hence, only quibbling interpretation, which is usually the philosophy of slavery, can confuse what eternal truth has distinguished by immutable relations.

After high treason come those crimes which violate the security of private persons. Since this is the chief end of every legitimate association, one cannot but assign some of the most considerable punishments established by law to the violation of the right to security which every citizen has.

The opinion that each citizen must have of being able to do anything that is not against the law without fearing any ill consequences save those that may flow from the action itself—this is the political dogma that the people should believe and that the highest magistrates should proclaim and keep with the same incorruptible care as the laws themselves.[3] This sacred dogma, without which there could be no legitimate society, is the just reward that men receive for sacrificing their total and universal freedom of action; such freedom is common to all sentient beings and is limited only by their own powers.[4] This dogma forms the free and vigorous spirit and the enlightened mind; it makes men virtuous, but with that sort of virtue that knows how to withstand fear, not with the submissive prudence that is worthy only of those who can tolerate a precarious and uncertain life. Attempts against the security and liberty of citizens, then, are among the greatest crimes. Under this heading fall not only murders and thefts committed by the common people, but also those committed by nobles and magistrates. Their influence works at a wider distance and with greater force, destroying the ideas of justice and duty among subjects and substituting the right of the strongest. This principle is just as dangerous to those who act on it as to those who suffer from it.

IX

HONOR

There is a remarkable contradiction between the civil laws, the jealous guardians of the person and property of each citizen above everything else, and the laws of what is called "honor," which gives preference to opinion. The term "honor" is one of those that has served as the basis for lengthy and brilliant discussions, though no fixed and stable idea has been attached to it. How miserable is the condition of the human mind! It has a better grasp of the most remote and least important ideas about the revolutions of the heavenly bodies than of the most immediate and important moral concepts, which are always fluctuating and confused as they are driven by the winds of passion and guided by the ignorance that receives and transmits them! This ostensible paradox will disappear, however, when one considers that, just as objects too close to one's eyes are blurred, so the excessive proximity of moral ideas makes it easy to confuse the large number of simple ideas that go to form them. Wishing to measure the phenomena of human sensibility, the geometric spirit needs dividing lines. When these are clearly drawn, the impartial observer of human affairs will be less astonished, and he will suspect that there is perhaps no need for so great a moral apparatus or for so many bonds in order to make men happy and secure.

"Honor," then, is one of those complex ideas that is an aggregate, not merely of simple ideas, but also of complex notions that, according to the various ways that they appear to the mind, sometimes admit and sometimes exclude some of their different constituent elements. They retain only a few common ideas, just as several complex algebraic quantities admit of only one common divisor. To find this common divisor among the various ideas that men have constructed about "honor," one must glance rapidly at the formation of societies. The first laws and the first magistrates were born of the necessity of redressing the disorders caused by the physical despotism of each man. This was the purpose for which society was founded, and this is the purpose that has always been retained, in fact or in appearance, at the head of all law codes, even destructive ones. The closer association of men and the progress of their understanding, however, gave birth to an infinite series of actions and reciprocal needs that always went beyond the immediate provisions of the law and yet that did not lie within the immediate power of each person to satisfy. The despotism of opinion dates from this epoch; opinion was the only means of obtaining from others those benefits and of preventing those evils for which the law did not sufficiently provide. It is opinion, moreover, that torments the sage and the unlettered alike, that has granted esteem more to the appearance of virtue than to virtue itself, and that makes even a rascal become a missionary since he finds this to be in his own interest. Hence, the esteem of men became not merely useful but necessary if one were not to fall below the common level. Hence, if the ambitious man strives to win it because it is useful, if the vain man begs for it as testimony to his own merit, one sees the man of honor demanding it as a necessity. This "honor" is a condition that a great many men place on their very existence. Since it was born after the establishment of society, it could not be placed in the common deposit of surrendered liberty that forms the sovereignty of a nation. It is, rather, a temporary return to the state of nature, a momentary withdrawal of one's person from those laws, that, in this case, do not provide a citizen with adequate protection.[1]

Hence, both in extreme political liberty and in extreme subjugation, ideas of honor disappear, or else they become entirely confused with other ideas; for, in the first case, the despotism of the laws makes it useless to seek the good opinion of others; in the second case, the despotism of men annihilates civil life and reduces everyone to having only a precarious and temporary personality. Honor is thus one of the fundamental principles of monarchies, which are a sort of attenuated despotism.[2] Honor has the same effect in them that revolutions do in despotic states: it serves as a temporary return to the state of nature, and, for the master, it is a reminder of the original equality of mankind.

X

DUELS

From this need for the esteem of others there arose private duels, which had their origin precisely in the anarchy of the law. It is said that duels were unknown in antiquity, perhaps because the ancients did not suspiciously arm themselves when gathering at temples or theatres or with their friends, perhaps because dueling was a commonplace and ignoble entertainment which enslaved and debased gladiators presented for the rabble, and free men disdained to be thought and called gladiators with their private battles. Edicts threatening death to anyone who accepts a challenge to a duel have vainly sought to extirpate this custom, which is founded on something that some men fear more than death. For, deprived of the good opinion of others, the man of honor foresees himself reduced to leading a purely solitary life (which is an intolerable condition for a sociable man), or else to becoming the target for insults and defamation, whose repeated actions carry greater weight with him than the danger of punishment. Why is it that the common people do not ordinarily fight duels as aristocrats do? It is not only because they are unarmed, but because the need for the esteem of others is less widespread among plebians than among those who, holding a more exalted station, regard one another with greater suspicion and jealousy.

It is not useless to repeat what others have written: namely, that the best method of preventing this crime is to punish the aggressor—that is, the person who has committed the offense that leads to a duel—and to declare innocent the man who, through no fault of his own, has been constrained to defend something that laws on the books do not assure to him, that is, the opinion which others hold of him; he has had to show his fellow citizens that he feared only the law and not men.[1]

21

XI

PUBLIC TRANQUILLITY

Finally, among crimes of the third type are those especially that disturb the public tranquillity and the peace of citizens: matters such as tumults and carousing in public thoroughfares meant for business and for traffic, or such as fanatical sermons that excite the fickle passions of the curious crowd. These passions gather strength from the great number of the audience; they owe more to the effects of a murky and mysterious rapture than to clear and calm reason, which never has any effect on a large mass of men.

Lighting towns by night at public expense; guards posted in various quarters of the city; the simple and moral discourses of religion confined to the silence and sacred calm of temples protected by the public authorities; speeches on behalf of private and public interests in national assemblies, parliaments, or any place that sovereign majesty resides—these are the effective means for preventing the dangerous concentration of popular passions. These things constitute an important branch of magisterial vigilance which the French call *la police*. If the magistrate acts according to arbitrary laws that are not established by a code that circulates among all citizens, however, then the door is open to tyranny, which is always at the frontiers of political freedom. I find no exception whatever to this general axiom: that every citizen must know when he is guilty and when he is innocent. If censors and arbitrary magistrates in general are necessary in certain regimes, this arises from the weakness of the constitution and not from the nature of a well-ordered government. Uncertainty regarding one's own fate has sacrificed more victims to secret tyranny than has public and official cruelty; the latter is repulsive rather than debasing to men's spirits. The real tyrant always begins by gaining control of opinion, thus forestalling courage. Courage can shine forth only in the clear light of truth, or in the fire of passion, or in ignorance of danger.

What punishments, then, will suit such crimes? Is death really a *useful* and *necessary* punishment for the security and good order of society? Are torture and instruments of torment *just*, and do they achieve the *end* for which laws are established? What is the best way to prevent crimes? Are the same punishments equally useful at all times? What influence do they have on

22

customs? These problems deserve a mathematically precise solution that the fog of sophistry, seductive eloquence, and timid doubt cannot withstand. If I were to have no other merit than to be the first person in Italy to present somewhat more clearly the things that other nations have dared to write and have begun to practice, I should deem myself fortunate,[1] but if, in the course of upholding the rights of men and invincible truth, I should contribute to saving an unhappy victim of tyranny or of equally pernicious ignorance from suffering and from the anguish of death, then the blessings and tears of that one person overcome with joy would console me for the contempt of all humanity.[2]

XII

PURPOSE
OF PUNISHMENTS

From the simple consideration of the truths expounded thus far, it is clear that the purpose of punishments is not to torment and afflict a sentient being or to undo a crime which has already been committed. Far from acting out of passion, can a political body, which is the calm agent that moderates the passions of private individuals, harbor useless cruelty, the tool of fury and fanaticism or of weak tyrants? Can the cries of a poor wretch turn back time and undo actions which have already been done? The purpose of punishment, then, is nothing other than to dissuade the criminal from doing fresh harm to his compatriots and to keep other people from doing the same. Therefore, punishments and the method of inflicting them should be chosen that, mindful of the proportion between crime and punishment, will make the most effective and lasting impression on men's minds and inflict the least torment on the body of the criminal.[1]

XIII

WITNESSES

It is a point of considerable importance in all good legislation to determine exactly the credibility of witnesses and the proofs of guilt. Every rational man, that is, everyone whose ideas have a certain coherence and whose sentiments are like those of other men, may be a witness. //The true measure of his credibility is simply the interest he has in telling or not telling the truth. Hence, it is apparent that excluding women from being witnesses because they are weak is frivolous, that treating condemned criminals as dead in fact because they are dead in law is puerile, and that insisting upon the infamy of the infamous is senseless when such persons have no interest in lying. // The credibility of a witness, therefore, must diminish in proportion to the hatred or friendship or close relationship between himself and the accused. More than one witness is necessary, for so long as the witness affirms the crime and the accused denies it, there is no certainty. What prevails in such a case is the right of everyone to be presumed innocent. The credibility of a witness diminishes significantly as the atrocity of the alleged crime increases* or as

//*Among experts in criminal law, the credibility of a witness becomes all the greater the more atrocious the crime is. Here is the iron maxim dictated by the most cruel stupidity: *In atrocissimis leviores coniecturae sufficiunt, et licit iudici iura transgredi.* Let us translate this into the vernacular, and Europeans will see one of the host of precepts, all equally "rational," to which they are subjected almost without knowing it: "In cases of the most atrocious crimes—that is, the least likely ones—the flimsiest conjectures are sufficient, and the judge is permitted to overstep the bounds of the law." [1] Absurd legal procedures are often produced by fear, which is the chief source of human contradictions. Frightened by the condemnation of an innocent person, legislators (who are really jurists to whom death has given the authority to pass judgment on everything and whom self-interested and venal writers have made the arbiters and legislators of human fortunes[2]) burden jurisprudence with superfluous formalities and exceptions, whose precise observation would seat anarchic impunity on the throne of justice. Frightened by a few terrible crimes that were difficult to prove, they felt constrained to evade the very formalities that they had established; so sometimes with despotic impatience, sometimes with effeminate timidity, they have transformed serious trials into a kind of game in which chance and subterfuge are the main elements.//

the circumstances become more improbable; witchcraft and gratuitously cruel acts are cases in point. In the former instance, it is more probable that several men are lying, for it is easier to believe that several men are deluded by ignorance and persecuting hatred than that a man exercises a power that God either did not give to or else took from every created being.[3] The same is true of the latter instance, for no man is cruel except in proportion to his self-interest, hatred, or imagined fear. Properly speaking, there is no superfluous sentiment in man; sentiment is always proportional to the result of the impressions made on the senses. Likewise, the credibility of a witness may be somewhat diminished if he is a member of some private society whose customs and maxims either are not well known or else are different from those of the general public. Such a man has not only his own passions, but those of others as well.[4]

Finally, the credibility of a witness is virtually nil when the case at hand involves making words a crime, for the tone, the gestures, and everything that precedes and follows the different ideas that men attach to the same terms alter and modify a person's remarks to such an extent that it is almost impossible to repeat them exactly as they were spoken.[5] Moreover, violent and extraordinary actions, which are real crimes, by their very nature leave traces behind them in a multitude of circumstances and consequences; words, however, remain only in the listeners' memory, something that is usually inaccurate and often corrupted. It is, then, far easier to slander someone's words than to slander his actions, for, in the latter case, the greater the number of circumstances adduced as evidence, the greater are the means available to the accused to clear himself.

XIV

/EVIDENCE AND
FORMS OF JUDGMENT

There is a general theorem that is very useful in calculating the certainty of a fact—for instance, the weight of evidence for a crime. When the proofs of a fact depend upon one another, that is, when different pieces of evidence are substantiated only by each other, then the more proofs that are adduced, the less likely the fact, for anything that would ruin the intial proofs would ruin the subsequent ones as well. //When all the proofs of a fact depend equally upon a single piece of evidence, the number of proofs neither augments nor diminishes the probability of the fact, for their total worth comes down to the worth of the one proof upon which they all depend.// When the proofs are independent of one another, that is, when the pieces of evidence are supported by something besides each other, then the likelihood of the fact increases as more proofs are adduced, because the flaws in one proof have no bearing on the others. I speak of probability in criminal cases, even though certainty ought to be required if punishment is to be inflicted. The paradox will vanish, however, for anyone who considers that, strictly speaking, moral certainty is only a sort of probability, but a probability such that it is deemed certainty, because everyone with good sense necessarily consents to it by dint of habit. Habit is born of the need to act, and it precedes any speculation. The certainty required to declare a person guilty, therefore, is the same as that which determines everyone in life's most important undertakings. //The proofs of a crime may be distinguished as perfect or imperfect. I call perfect those proofs that exclude the possibility that a given person may be innocent; I call imperfect those that do not exclude it. A single proof of the first sort is sufficient for conviction; of the second sort, as many are required as are needed to form one perfect proof; that is to say, though each one by itself does not exclude the possibility of innocence, taken together on the same subject they exclude it absolutely. One must note that imperfect proofs of which the accused could clear himself become perfect if he fails to do so in a satisfactory way. It is easier to feel this moral certainty of proofs, though, than it is to define it exactly.// For this reason, I think it an excellent law that establishes assessors or assistants to the chief judge who are chosen by lot rather than hand-picked, for in this instance ignorance, which judges by feeling, is more reliable than learning, which judges by opinion. Where the laws are clear and precise, the duty of the judge is simply to ascertain the fact. If the investigation of a crime demands ability and skill, if the presentation of the findings requires clarity and precision, judging the results of the investigation themselves demands only plain common sense, which is less subject to error than the erudition of a judge who is accustomed to finding people guilty and who reduces everything to an artificial system borrowed from his studies. Happy the nation where law is not a science! It is a most useful law that every man be judged by his peers, for, when the liberty and fortune of a citizen are at stake, those sentiments which inequality inspires should fall silent.[1] The superiority with which the fortunate man looks down upon the unfortunate and the disdain with which an inferior regards his superior can have no place in this judgment. When the crime is an offense against a third party, however, then half the jurors should be the equals of the accused and half the peers of the victim. Thus, all private interests that might alter the appearance of things (albeit involuntarily) are balanced, and only the law and the truth are heard. Further, it is in accord with justice that the accused should be able to exclude up to a certain number of jurors from his case if he has any suspicion about them. If he is permitted to use this right for a time without restraint and does so, he will almost seem to condemn himself. Let verdicts and proofs of guilt be public, so that opinion, which is perhaps the only cement holding society together, may impose a restraint on force and passions, and so that the common people may say, "We are not slaves, and we are protected." This sentiment inspires courage, and it is worth as much as taxes to a sovereign who understands his true interests. I shall not go into other details and precautions that such institutions require. Were it necessary to say everything, I should have said nothing./

XV

SECRET ACCUSATIONS[1]

Secret accusations are an evident but time-honored abuse made necessary in many nations by the weakness of the constitution. Such a custom makes men false and dissimulating. Anyone who can suspect another person of being an informer sees in him an enemy. Men then grow accustomed to masking their personal feelings, and, through the habit of hiding them from others, they end by hiding their sentiments from themselves. How unhappy men are when they reach this point! Without clear and firm principles to guide them, they wander bewildered and aimless in the vast sea of opinions, always concerned with saving themselves from the monsters which threaten them. Their present is always embittered by the uncertainty of their future. Deprived of the lasting pleasures of tranquillity and security, only a scant few happy moments scattered here and there in their sad lives and devoured in haste and disorder console them for having been alive. And shall we make of such men the bold soldiers who defend the country and the throne? Among these men shall we find the uncorrupted magistrates who sustain and enlarge the true interests of the sovereign with free and patriotic eloquence, who bring tribute to the throne together with the love and blessings of all classes of men, giving in return to palaces and hovels alike peace, security, and the industrious hope of bettering one's lot, which is the useful leaven and the very life of states?

Who can defend himself against calumny when it is armed with tyranny's strongest shield, *secrecy*? What on earth is the form of government in which the ruler suspects every subject of being an enemy and, in order to assure the public peace, deprives each citizen of tranquillity?

/What are the reasons with which people justify secret accusations and punishments? The public welfare? The security and maintenance of the established form of government? What a strange constitution it must be in which the regime that controls force and public opinion (which is even stronger than force) fears every citizen! The safety of the accuser? The laws, then, do not suffice to defend him; one must conclude that there are subjects stronger than the sovereign! The infamy of the informer? Then slander is permitted when it is secret and punished when it is public! The nature of the crime? If harmless actions, or even acts useful to the public, are deemed crimes, then accusations and judgments can never be secret enough! Can there be crimes—that is, offenses against the public—when at the same time it is not in everyone's interest to have a public example and, hence, a public judgment? I respect every government, and I am not speaking of any one in particular. Sometimes circumstances are such that one can believe that the extirpation of an evil inherent in the system of government would mean the complete ruin of the state. But if I had to dictate laws in some deserted corner of the universe, my hand would tremble before I authorized such a custom, and I would see all posterity before my eyes./ Monsieur de Montesquieu has already said that public accusations are better suited to a republic, where the public good ought to be the strongest passion of the citizens, than to a monarchy, where this passion is greatly weakened by the very nature of the government. There it is best to establish appointed commissioners who accuse lawbreakers in the name of the people.[2] But every regime, republican and monarchical alike, should inflict upon the false accuser the same punishment that the accused would have received.

XVI

TORURE[1]

The torture of the accused while his trial is still in progress is a cruel practice sanctioned by the usage of most nations. Its purpose is either to make the accused confess his crime, or to resolve the contradictions into which he has fallen, or to discover his accomplices, or to purge him of infamy for some metaphysical and incomprehensible reason or other, /or, finally, to find out other crimes of which he may be guilty but of which he is not accused./

A man cannot be called "guilty" before the judge has passed sentence, and society cannot withdraw its protection except when it has been determined that he has violated the contracts on the basis of which that protection was granted to him. What right, then, other than the right of force, gives a judge the power to inflict punishment on a citizen while the question of his guilt or innocence is still in doubt? This dilemma is not new: either the crime is certain, or it is not; if it is certain, then no other punishment is suitable for the criminal except the one established by law, and torture is useless because the confession of the accused is unnecessary; if the crime is uncertain, one should not torment an innocent person, for, in the eyes of the law, he is a man whose misdeeds have not been proven.[2] But I add, moreover, that one confuses all natural relationships in requiring a man to be the accuser and the accused at the same time and in making pain the crucible of truth, as though the criterion of truth lay in the muscles and fibers of a poor wretch. This is a sure way to acquit robust scoundrels and to condemn weak but innocent people. This criterion is worthy of a cannibal, and the Romans (who were themselves barbarians on more than one count) kept it only for slaves, the victims of a ferocious and overpraised "virtue."

What is the political goal of punishment? It is to intimidate others. But what justification can we give, then, for the secret and private carnage that the tyranny of custom wreaks on the guilty and the innocent? It is important that no manifest crime go unpunished, but it is useless to discover who has committed a crime that lies buried in darkness. A wrong which has already been done and for which there is no remedy cannot be punished by political society except when the failure to do so would arouse false hopes of impunity in others. If it is true that more men, whether from virtue or fear, respect the law than violate it, then the risk of torturing an innocent person should be considered all the greater when, other things being equal, the probability is greater that a man has respected the law rather than despised it.

Another ridiculous reason for torture is the purgation of infamy; that is, a man judged infamous by law must confirm his deposition with the dislocation of his bones.[3] This abuse should not be tolerated in the eighteenth century. The underlying belief is that pain, which is a sensation, purges infamy, which is simply a moral relationship. Is pain perhaps a crucible? And is infamy perhaps a mixed and impure substance? It is not difficult to go back to the origin of this ridiculous law, since the very absurdities adopted by a whole nation always have some relationship to the common and respected ideas of that nation. This custom seems to be taken from religious and spiritual ideas which have so much influence on the thoughts of men, nations, and ages. An infallible dogma assures us that the blemishes which result from human weakness and which yet have not deserved the eternal wrath of the Great Being must be purged with an incomprehensible fire. Now infamy is a civil blemish, and, since pain and fire remove spiritual and disembodied stains, will the spasms of torture not remove a civil stain, namely infamy? I believe that the confession of the criminal, which certain courts require for conviction, has an analogous origin, for, in the mysterious tribunal of penance, the confession of sins is an essential part of the sacrament. This is how men abuse the very clear light of revelation. Just as such light is the only one that still shines in times of ignorance, so docile humanity runs to it on every occasion, giving it the most absurd and far-fetched applications.[4] Infamy, however, is a sentiment that is not subject to reason or to law, but to public opinion. Torture itself causes real infamy for its victim. Hence, this method seeks to remove infamy by inflicting it.

The third pretext is that suspects should be tortured when they have contradicted themselves during their examination—as though the fear of punishment, the uncertainty of the verdict, the pomp and majesty of the tribunal, the ignorance common to almost all scoundrels and innocent persons, did not make self-contradiction likely, both for the innocent party in fear and for the criminal trying to dissimulate; as though contradictions, which are common enough among calm men, would not be multiplied in the turbulent mind of someone completely absorbed in the thought of saving himself from immediate danger.

This infamous crucible of truth is an enduring monument to the ancient and savage legislation of an age when ordeals by fire and boiling water and the uncertain outcome of armed combat were called "judgments of God"—as though the links of the eternal chain which is in the bosom of the First Cause had to be disordered and disconnected at every moment for the sake of frivolous human arrangements. The only difference between torture and ordeals by fire and boiling water is that the outcome of the former seems to depend on the will of the accused, while the result of the latter depends on a purely physical and external fact. This difference, however, is apparent rather than real. Speaking the truth amid convulsions and torments is no more a free act than staving off the effects of fire and boiling water except by fraud. Every act of our will is always proportional to the strength of the sense impressions from which it springs, and the sensory capacity of every man is limited. Thus, the sensation of pain may increase to such a point that, filling the entire mind of the victim, it leaves him no liberty but to choose the shortest route to ending the pain for the time being.[5] Under such conditions, the reply of the accused is as inevitable as the impressions of fire or water, and the sensitive innocent person will declare himself guilty if he believes that by so doing he can put an end to his torment. Every difference between the guilty and the innocent disappears with the use of the very means allegedly employed to discover it. /It is superfluous to shed further light on the subject by citing the innumerable examples of innocent persons who confessed themselves guilty because of the agonies of torture. There is no nation and there is no age from which such cases might not be cited, but men neither change nor draw the obvious conclusion. There is no man who, having raised his thoughts above the necessities of life, has not at times hurried toward Nature, who calls him to her with secret and indistinct voices, but custom, that tyrant of minds, pushes him back and intimidates him./ The outcome of torture, then, is a matter of temperament and calculation that varies with each man in proportion to his hardiness and his sensitivity, so that, by means of this method, a mathematician could solve the following problem better than a judge could: given the strength of an innocent person's muscles and the sensitivity of his fibers, find the degree of pain that will make him confess himself guilty of a given crime.[6]

The examination of someone accused of a crime is undertaken in order to learn the truth, but, if truth is difficult to discover in the bearing, the gestures, and the expression of a calm man, all the less will one find it in a man in whom the convulsions of pain have distorted all the signs by which the truth reveals itself on the faces of most men in spite of themselves. Every violent action confounds and annihilates the tiny differences in objects by which one may sometimes distinguish truth from falsehood.

These truths were recognized by Roman legislators, according to whom the use of torture was restricted entirely to slaves, who had been stripped of all legal personality.[7] These truths are appreciated among the legislators of England, a nation whose literary glory, whose superiority in commerce and wealth (and hence in power), and whose examples of virtue and courage leave no doubt as to the excellence of its laws.[8] Torture has been abolished in Sweden.[9] It has been abolished by one of the wisest monarchs in Europe who, having brought philosophy to the throne and being a legislator who loves his subjects, has made them equal and free in their common dependence on the law; this, given the current state of affairs, is the only equality and freedom that reasonable men can demand.[10] Torture is not deemed necessary in military law, although armed forces are in large measure made up of the dregs of nations and would seem on that account to need it more than any other group. It is strange, if one does not consider how great the tyranny of custom is, that the laws of peace must learn the most humane method of judgment from souls hardened to slaughter and bloodshed.

Finally, this truth is felt, albeit in a confused manner, by those very persons who are removed from it: a confession made under torture is of no value unless it is confirmed by oath after the torture had ended. If the accused does not confirm his guilt, however, he is tortured again.[11] Some learned jurists and some nations permit this infamous sort of question-begging only three times; other nations and other learned jurists leave the matter to the discretion of the judge. The upshot is that of two men equally innocent or equally guilty, the vigorous and bold one will be saved and the weak and timid one condemned by virtue of this rigorous line of reasoning: "I, the judge, had to find you guilty of a certain crime. You, stout fellow, were able to withstand the pain, and hence I acquit you. You, weakling, have given in, and therefore I condemn you. I feel that the confession extracted from you amid torments ought to be invalid, but I shall torture you anew if you do not confirm what you have confessed."

A strange consequence that necessarily follows from the use of torture is that the innocent person is placed in a worse situation than the criminal, since if both of them are tortured, all circumstances are against the former: for either he confesses to the crime and is condemned, or else he is found innocent after having suffered a punishment that he did not deserve. The criminal, on the other hand, is in an inherently favorable situation: that is, if he firmly withstands the torture, he is acquitted; he has exchanged a greater punishment for a lesser one. Thus, the innocent cannot but lose, and the guilty can only gain.

The law establishing torture is a law that declares: "Men, resist pain, and, if Nature has created in you an inextinguishable self-love, if she has given you an inalienable right to defend yourselves, I create in you a completely different sentiment: an heroic self-contempt. Further, I command you to accuse yourselves, speaking the truth even while your muscles are being sprained and your bones dislocated."

/Torture is employed to discover whether the accused is guilty of crimes other than the one with which he is charged. This is equivalent to the following line of reasoning: "You are guilty of one crime; hence it is possible that you are guilty of a hundred others. This doubt weighs on me, and I want to reassure myself by using my criterion for truth. The law torments you because you are guilty, because you may be guilty, because I want you to be guilty."/

Finally, an accused person is tortured in order to discover his partners in crime. Since it has already been shown that this is not an effective means of determining the truth, how can it serve to unmask accomplices, which is one of the truths to be found out?[12] As though a man who accuses himself would not accuse others more readily. Besides, is it just to torment men for the crimes of others? Will accomplices not be discovered by the examination of witnesses, the interrogation of the accused, the evidence and the facts of the crime—in short, by all of the same means employed to find the accused guilty of the crime? For the most part, accomplices flee at once after the capture of their companion. The uncertainty of their fate in itself condemns them to exile and frees the country from the danger of further offenses, while the punishment of the criminal who is in chains attains its one true goal: to deter other men by fear from committing a similar crime.

XVII

//THE PUBLIC TREASURY

There was once a time when practically all punishments were fines. The crimes that men committed were the patrimony of the prince.[1] Attempts against the public security were a source of profit, and whoever was charged with defending it had an interest in seeing it violated. The object of punishment was thus a contest between the treasury (which collected the fines) and the criminal. This was a civil, contentious, and private matter rather than a public one, and it gave the treasury rights other than those conferred by the defense of society; it also inflicted on the criminal other wrongs than the punishments needed in order to set an example. Hence, the judge was an advocate for the treasury rather than an impartial seeker after truth, a revenue agent as well as the defender and minister of the law. With this system, however, to confess oneself guilty was tantamount to confessing oneself a debtor of the treasury, which was the purpose of criminal proceedings at that time, and the confession of guilt, framed so as to favor the interests of the treasury and not to injure them, became and still is (effects always continue a long time after the causes have ceased) the pivot on which all criminal jurisprudence turns. Without this confession, a criminal convicted by unquestioned evidence will suffer a lighter punishment than the legally established one; without it, he will not be tortured in order to discover other crimes of the same sort that he might have committed. With such a confession, however, the judge takes possession of the criminal's body and tears him apart with methodical formality in order to extract, as from acquired property, all the profit he can. Once the occurrence of the crime is established, the confession constitutes a convincing proof, and, to make it less suspect, it is extracted by force with the agonies and desperation of pain. At the same time, a calm, indifferent, extrajudicial confession, unaffected by the overwhelming fears of a trial by torture, does not suffice to convict a criminal. Investigations and proofs which shed light on the case but damage revenue interests are disregarded. It is not out of concern for misery and weakness that the accused is sometimes spared torments, but out of concern for losses that this entity, which is nowadays so imaginary and inconceivable, might suffer. The judge becomes the enemy of the accused, of a man in chains, a man who is a prey to squalor, torments, and a most terrible future. The judge does not seek the truth of the case; he seeks the prisoner's guilt and lays traps for him, and, if these snares fail, he deems himself personally defeated; he thinks that his infallibility, which man arrogates to himself in all things, has been undermined. This is what is called an "offensive proceeding," and such are the criminal trials almost everywhere in enlightened Europe in the eighteenth century. The real trial, the "informative" one, that is, the impartial investigation of facts which reason demands, which military law uses, and which even Asiatic despotism practices in simple and trivial cases, is very little used in European tribunals. What a complicated labyrinth of strange absurdities which a happier posterity will undoubtedly find incredible! Only philosophers of that future time will see, by studying human nature, that such a system was ever possible.//

XVIII

OATHS

A contradiction between the law and natural human feelings arises since the oaths, which are required of an accused person, are administered to him so that he will tell the truth, although he has every reason to lie—as though a man could bind himself to contribute to his own destruction; as though religion did not fall silent in most men when self-interest speaks.[1] The experience of all ages has shown that men abuse this precious gift of heaven more than anything else. And why will scoundrels respect it if those men who are deemed the most virtuous have often flouted it? For most people, the motives that religion opposes to the tumult of fear and the love of life are too weak because they are too remote. The affairs of heaven are ruled by laws altogether different from those which govern human affairs. Why should they be used to compromise one another? And why place a man in the terrible dilemma of either failing God or of being a party to his own ruin? The law that requires such an oath, then, demands that one be a bad Christian or else a martyr. Little by little, the oath becomes a mere formality, thereby destroying the strength of religious sentiments, the only guarantee of the honesty of most men. Experience has shown how useless oaths are, for any judge can be my witness that no oath has ever made any criminal tell the truth. Reason shows how useless oaths are, for it declares that all laws which conflict with natural human feelings are useless and consequently dangerous. The same thing happens to such laws as to dikes built in direct opposition to the main current of a river: either they are destroyed and washed away at once, or else a whirlpool that they themselves create erodes and undermines them imperceptibly.

XIX

PROMPTNESS
OF PUNISHMENT

The more prompt the punishment is and the sooner it follows the crime, the more just and useful it will be. I say more just, because it spares the criminal the useless and cruel torments of uncertainty, which grow with the vigor of one's imagination and the sense of one's own weakness; more just, because being deprived of one's liberty is a punishment, and this cannot precede the sentence except when necessity demands it. Imprisonment, then, simply means taking someone into custody until he is found guilty, and, as such custody is essentially punitive, it should last as short a time as possible and be as lenient as possible. The duration of imprisonment should be determined both by the time necessary for the trial and by the right of those who have been detained the longest to be tried first. The rigor of detention must not exceed what is necessary to forestall escape or the concealment of evidence. The trial itself must be completed in the shortest possible time. Can there be a more cruel contrast than the one between the indolence of a judge and the anguish of someone accused of a crime—between the comforts and pleasures of an unfeeling magistrate on the one hand, and, on the other, the tears and squalid condition of a prisoner? In general, the burden of a punishment and the consequence of a crime should have the greatest impact on others and yet be as mild as possible for the person who suffers it; for one cannot call any society "legitimate" if it does not recognize as an indisputable principle that men have wanted to subject themselves only to the least possible evils.

I have said that promptness of punishment is more useful, for the less time that passes between the misdeed and its chastisement, the stronger and more permanent is the human mind's association of the two ideas of *crime* and *punishment,* so that imperceptibly the one will come to be considered as the cause and the other as the necessary and inevitable result. It is well established that the association of ideas is the cement that shapes the whole structure of the human intellect; without it, pleasure and pain would be isolated feelings with no consequences. The farther removed men are from general ideas and universal principles—in other words, the more uneducated

36

men are—the more they act on the basis of immediate and very familiar associations, neglecting the more remote and complicated ones. The latter are useful only to men strongly impassioned for the object after which they are striving. The light of their attention illuminates this one object only, leaving all others in darkness. Such remote and complicated associations are likewise useful to more lofty minds, for they have acquired the habit of rapidly surveying many objects at once, and they have the ability to contrast many partial sentiments with one another, so that the outcome, which is action, is less dangerous and uncertain.

The temporal proximity of crime and punishment, then, is of the utmost importance if one desires to arouse in crude and uneducated minds the idea of punishment in association with the seductive image of a certain advantageous crime. Long delay only serves to disconnect those two ideas, and whatever impression the chastisement of a crime may make, /that impression will be made more as a spectacle than a punishment./ Further, the impression will come only after the horror of a given crime, which ought to reinforce the feeling of punishment, has grown weak in the minds of the spectators.

Another principle serves admirably to tighten even further the connection between the misdeed and its punishment, namely, that the latter should conform as closely as possible to the nature of the crime. This analogy marvelously facilitates the contrast that should exist between the motive for a crime and the consequent impact of punishment, so that the latter draws the mind away and leads it to quite a different end than the one toward which the seductive idea of breaking the law seeks to direct it.

XX

CRIMES

OF VIOLENCE

Crimes against persons are one thing, and crimes against property are another. Without exception the former should be punished with corporal penalties.[1] Neither the great nor the rich should be able to atone for an attempt against the weak and the poor by means of a cash payment. Otherwise riches, which, under the supervision of the law, are the reward of industry, become the food of tyranny. There is no liberty whenever the law in some cases permits a man to cease to be a *person* and to become a *thing*.[2] Then you will see the efforts of the powerful man directed entirely to drawing whatever may legally be to his own advantage from every possible social arrangement. This discovery is the magic secret that transforms citizens into beasts of burden; in the hands of the strong, it is the chain with which he binds the actions of the unwary and the weak. This is why, in some regimes that have all the appearance of liberty, tyranny lies hidden, or insinuates itself into some corner neglected by the legislator, where it subtly gathers strength and grows. For the most part, men erect the most solid dikes against overt tryanny, but they do not see the imperceptible insect that gnaws those dikes and opens a path for the invading flood, a path that is all the more secure because it is more concealed.

XXI

/PUNISHMENT
OF NOBLES

What, then, shall the punishments assigned to the crimes of nobles, whose privileges constitute a large part of the laws of various nations? I shall not examine here if this hereditary distinction between nobles and commoners be useful in a regime or necessary in a monarchy; nor shall I examine if it be true that this distinction forms an intermediary power that limits the excesses of the two extremes, or if it does not; rather, create a class that is enslaved to itself and to others and that, like the fertile and agreeable oases standing out among the vast, sandy deserts of Arabia, restricts the circulation of reputation and hope within a very narrow circle.[1] Neither shall I examine whether, granting inequality to be inevitable or useful in societies, it should also be the case that this inequality ought to be established among classes rather than individuals, limited to one area rather than circulating throughout the whole body politic, or self-perpetuating rather than constantly being renewed and abolished. I shall confine myself entirely to the punishments that nobles deserve, maintaining that they should be the same for the first citizen as for the least. In order to be legitimate, every distinction, whether it be in honor or wealth, presupposes an anterior equality founded upon the law, which considers all subjects as equally dependent upon itself. One must assume that men who have given up their natural despotism have said, "Let whoever is most industrious have the greatest honor, and let his fame shine upon his successors; but though the person who is happier or more honored may hope for more, let him fear no less than others to violate those convenants by means of which he is raised above his fellows."[2] It is true that such decrees never issued from a parliament of the human race, but they do exist in the immutable relationships of things. They do not destroy those advantages that nobility supposedly produces, and they prevent its ill effects. They make the law formidable, closing every avenue to impunity. If anyone should say that the same punishment inflicted on a noble and a commoner is not really the same because of the difference in upbringing and because of the infamy spattered on an illustrious family, I should reply that the sensitivity of the criminal is not the measurement of punishment, but rather the public injury, which is all the greater when it is done by one whom society has favored; that equality of punishment can only be extrinsic, for it is really different for each individual; and that the sovereign can remove a family's disgrace by public demonstrations of benevolence toward a criminal's relatives.[3] And isn't it common knowledge that such formal displays take the place of reason for the credulous and admiring crowd?/

XXII

THEFTS

A theft that is not accompanied by violence ought to be punished with a fine. Whoever seeks to enrich himself with the property of others ought to be deprived of his own. Ordinarily, however, theft is only the crime of misery and desperation; it is the crime of that unhappy portion of humanity to whom the

right of property—a terrible and perhaps unnecessary right—has left only a
bare existence.[1] /Further, monetary punishments increase the number of
criminals over and above the number of crimes, taking bread away from the
innocent in taking it away from the guilty. The most fitting punishment,/ then,
is the only sort of slavery that can be deemed just: the temporary subjugation
to society of the labor and the person of the criminal, so that by his complete
personal dependence he may make restitution for his unjust and despotic en-
croachment against the social contract. When theft is accompanied by
violence, however, the chastisement should be an equal mixture of penal servitude and bodily punishment.[2] Other writers before me have demonstrated
the evident abuse of using the same punishments for violent robberies and for
those committed entirely by fraud; such an abuse absurdly equates a huge
sum of money with a man's life.[3] It is never superfluous, though, to repeat
something that has hardly ever been put into practice. Political machines
more than any others retain their initial motion, and they are the slowest to
move in a new direction. Violent robbery and theft by fraud are of different
natures, and, even in politics, this mathematical axiom is most certain: that infinity separates heterogeneous quantities.

XXIII

INFAMY

Personal injuries that are contrary to honor—that is, to the just measure of
esteem that a citizen is entitled to demand from others—ought to be punished
with infamy. Such disgrace is a sign of public disapproval, depriving the
criminal of general consideration, of the confidence of his country, and of that
almost fraternal feeling which society inspires. Infamy of this sort does not fall
within the purview of the law. It is necessary, then, that legal disgrace should
coincide with the infamy that arises from the relationships of things, the same
as that which comes from universal morality or from a specific morality built
upon particular systems that rule common opinion in a given nation.[1] If legal
infamy departs from universal or particular ideas of morality, either the law
loses public esteem, or else notions of probity and morality vanish altogether

despite declamations, which can never stand up to the impact of examples. Anyone who declares that certain acts are infamous when they are in themselves morally indifferent diminishes the infamy of actions that really are disgraceful. Punishments involving infamy should neither be used too frequently nor fall upon a great many people at once: not the former, for the continual and too frequent effects of matters of opinion weaken the force of opinion itself; not the latter, for the disgrace of many comes down to the disgrace of no one.

//Painful corporal punishments should not be assigned to such crimes; they are founded on pride, and they draw glory and nourishment from pain itself. Ridicule and shame are appropriate for such crimes, punishments which check the vanity of fanatics with the vanity of the spectators, punishments over whose tenacity truth itself can scarcely triumph with slow and obstinate efforts. Thus, by using force against force and opinion against opinion, the wise legislator overcomes the admiration and surprise aroused in the mob by a false principle. The accurately deduced consequences of such a principle are likely to hide its original absurdity from the uneducated.//

This is the way to avoid confusing immutable relationships and the very nature of things; not limited by time and operating incessantly, they upset and undo all limited regulations that depart from them. The faithful imitation of nature is not the universal principle of the arts of taste and pleasure alone. The political art itself—politics of the true and lasting sort, at any rate—falls under this general maxim, for it is nothing other than the art of better directing and harmonizing immutable human feelings.[2]

XXIV

POLITICAL IDLENESS

Anyone who disturbs the public peace, who does not obey the laws—that is, the conditions by which men support one another and defend themselves—must be excluded from society; in other words, he must be banished. This is the reason why wise governments to do not permit political idleness in the midst of work and industry. Stern moralists confuse such idleness with the leisure born of riches, a leisure that is necessary and useful to the extent that society has expanded and administration has become centralized. I call political indolence the sort that contributes to society neither with work nor with wealth and that always acquires but never parts with its money. Although the common crowd venerates it with stupid admiration, the wise man looks upon it with disdainful compassion for the beings who are its victims. Having no need to conserve or increase the necessities of life, which is the stimulus to an active existence, their idleness allows full scope to their passions of opinion, which are by no means the weakest.[1] A person is not indolent in the political sense if he enjoys the fruits of the vices or virtues of his own ancestors and if he offers bread and livelihood to industrious poverty in exchange for his immediate pleasures. A person is not politically idle if he uses wealth to carry on the quiet war of industry instead of using force to wage uncertain and bloody campaigns.[2] And thus the laws, rather than the austere and limited virtue of a few censors, ought to define what sort of idleness should be punished.

//It seems that banishment should be imposed on those who have been accused of an atrocious crime and whose guilt is probable, though not certain. For this, however, a statute is needed that is as little arbitrary and as precise as possible, a statute that condemns to banishment anyone who has placed the nation in the fatal dilemma of fearing him or of punishing him unjustly. Nevertheless, the law should leave him the sacred right of proving his innocence. The motives should be greater against a foreigner than a citizen, against a person indicted for the first time than a recidivist.//

XXV

BANISHMENT
AND CONFISCATIONS

But should someone who has been banished and excluded forever from the society of which he was a member be deprived of his property? Such a question may be considered under different aspects. The loss of one's possessions is a punishment greater than banishment; thus, there are cases in which, depending on the crime, the criminal should forfeit all of his possessions, or some of them, or none. Confiscation will be total when the banishment decreed by law is such that it completely destroys the relations between society and a delinquent citizen; in such an instance, the citizen dies even though the man remains alive, and, as far as the body politic is concerned, this should produce the same effect as natural death. It would appear, then, that all the criminal's property should pass to his legitimate successors rather than to the prince, for death and banishment of this sort are one and the same with regard to the body politic.[1] It is not because of this subtlety, however, that I dare to disapprove of confiscations of a criminal's possessions. If some people have maintained that such forfeitures are a check on vendettas and the arrogance of private individuals, they fail to consider that, even if punishments produce a happy result, they are not always therefore just, for, in order to be just, they must be necessary. A useful injustice cannot be tolerated by any legislator who wants to close every door to vigilant tyranny.[2] Tyranny deceives us with temporary good results and with the happiness of a few illustrious persons, paying no heed to future disasters or to the tears of a multitude of obscure people. Confiscations put a price on the head of the weak, cause the innocent to suffer the punishment of the guilty, and place the innocent themselves in the desperate necessity of committing crimes. Could there be a sorrier spectacle than that of a family dragged into shame and misery by the crimes of its head, crimes that the submission ordained by law would hinder the family from preventing, even if there were a way of doing so?

XXVI

THE SPIRIT
OF THE FAMILY[1]

Such pernicious and authorized injustices have been approved even by the most enlightened men and practiced in the freest republics because society has been considered as a union of families rather than as a union of individuals.[2] Suppose there are a hundred-thousand people, or twenty-thousand families, each composed of five persons, including the head who represents it: if the association be made up of families, there will be twenty-thousand men and eighty-thousand slaves; if the association be one of persons, there will be a hundred-thousand citizens and no slaves at all. In the former case, there will be a republic made up of twenty-thousand little monarchies; in the latter case, a republican spirit will breathe not only in the public forums and assemblies of the nation, but even within the walls of private homes, where men find a great deal of their happiness or misery. As laws and customs are the result of the habitual sentiments of the members of a commonwealth, in the former case, where the members are heads of households, a monarchical spirit will make its way little by little into the republic itself, and its effects will be checked merely by conflicting individual interests, certainly not by a sentiment that breathes liberty and equality. The spirit of the family is a spirit of details; it is confined to trivial facts. The spirit that rules republics is a master of general principles; it sees facts and combines them under broad and important categories for the sake of the good of the majority. In the republic composed of families, the children remain under the power of the head of the household as long as he lives, and they must wait for his death before they can lead a life dependent only on the laws. Accustomed to submission and fear in the full strength of their youth, when their feelings are least attenuated by that timidity born of experience which is called "moderation," how will they resist the obstacles that vice always puts in the way of virtue once they reach their feeble and declining old age, when any vigorous reform is checked by the lack of hope of seeing the results?

When the republic is made up of persons, familial subordination is not based on imposed authority but on contract, and the children become free members of the commonwealth when maturity frees them from the natural dependence that comes from weakness and the need for education and protection. They submit themselves to the head of the family in order to participate in its advantages, just as free men do in the larger family of civil society. In the republic composed of families, the children—which is to say, the most numerous and most useful part of the nation—are under the arbitrary control of their fathers. In the commonwealth made up of individuals, the only binding command is the sacred and inviolable duty of rendering one another all necessary assistance and, moreover, the obligation of showing gratitude for benefits received. Such bonds are destroyed not so much by the malice of the human heart as by an ill-conceived subjugation decreed by law.[3]

Such contradictions between family law and the fundamental laws of the republic are a fertile source of further contradictions between domestic and public morality; therefore, they give rise to a perpetual conflict in everyone's mind. Authoritarian family law inspires subjugation and fear; the principles of a republic inspire courage and liberty. The former teaches people to confine their devotion to a small number of persons whom they have not even chosen freely; the latter demand that such devotion be extended to all classes of men. The former demands constant self-sacrifice to a vain idol called "the good of the family," which frequently is not the good of any family member; the latter teaches a citizen to serve his own interests without offending the law, or it inspires him to patriotic self-destruction with the reward of zeal that precedes action. Such contradictions make men scorn the pursuit of virtue. They find virtue to be hidden, confused, and removed from themselves by the sort of distance that the obscurity of physical or moral objects entails. How many times a man recalling his past actions is astounded by his dishonesty! As the population of a society grows, each member becomes a smaller part of the whole, and republican sentiment diminishes accordingly if the laws do not take care to reinforce it. Societies, like human bodies, have their circumscribed limits, and, if they grow beyond these limits, their structure is necessarily disturbed. It seems that the size of a state must be in inverse proportion to the patriotic sentiment of its members. Otherwise, if the state's population and territory grow together, sound laws will find an obstacle to preventing crimes in the very good that they themselves have produced.[4] A republic that is too vast can save itself from despotism only by subdividing itself into several federated republics. But how can this be achieved? By a despotic dictator with the courage of Sulla and with as much genius for building up as Sulla had for destroying. If such a man be ambitious, the glory of all ages awaits him; if he be a philosopher, the blessings of his fellow citizens will console him for his loss of authority, assuming that he has not grown indifferent to their ingratitude.[5] To the extent that the feelings uniting a nation grow weaker, attachments to surrounding objects grow stronger. This is why friendships are strongest and most enduring in a despotic state, and family virtues, which are always mediocre, are the most common, or rather the only ones. From all this, anyone can see how limited the outlook of most legislators has been.

XXVII

MILDNESS
OF PUNISHMENTS

But my train of thought has taken me away from my subject, and I hasten to return in order to clarify it. One of the greatest checks on crime is not the cruelty of punishments but their inevitability. Consequently, in order to be effective, virtues, magisterial vigilance and inexorable judicial severity must be accompanied by mild legislation. The certainty of a chastisement, even if it be moderate, will always make a greater impression than the fear of a more terrible punishment that is united with the hope of impunity; for, when they are certain, even the least of evils always terrifies men's minds, while hope, that heavenly gift that often fills us completely, always removes from us the idea of worse punishments, especially if that hope is reinforced by the examples of impunity which weakness and greed frequently accord. The very savagery of a punishment makes the criminal all the bolder in taking risks to avoid it precisely because the evil with which he is threatened is so great, so much so that he commits several crimes in order to escape the punishment for a single one of them. The countries and ages in which punishments have been most atrocious have always been the scene of the bloodiest and most inhuman actions, for the same spirit of ferocity that guided the hand of the legislator governed the hand of the parricide and the assassin. Seated on the throne, this spirit dictated iron laws for savage and slavish souls to obey; in private darkness, it moved men to destory one tyrant in order to create another.[1]

To the degree that punishments become more cruel, men's souls become hardened, just as fluids always seek the level of surrounding objects, and the constantly active force of the passions leads to this: after a hundred years of cruel punishments, breaking on the wheel[2] occasions no more fright than imprisonment did at first. In order for a penalty to achieve its objective, all that is required is that the harm of the punishment should exceed the benefit resulting from the crime. Further, the inevitability of the punishment and the loss of the anticipated advantage of the crime should enter into this calculation of the excess of harm.[3] Everything more than this is thus superfluous and therefore tyrannical. Men regulate their conduct by the

46

repeated experience of evils which they know, not by those of which they are ignorant. Let us imagine two nations, each having a scale of punishments proportional to crimes; in one, the maximum penalty is perpetual slavery, and, in the other, breaking on the wheel. I maintain that the first nation will have as much fear of its greatest punishment as the second.[4] If for some reason the first of these nations were to adopt the more severe penalties of the second, the same reason might lead the latter to increase its punishments, passing gradually from breaking on the wheel to slower and more deliberate torments, and finally to the ultimate refinements of that science that tyrants know all too well.

Cruelty of punishments leads to two other ruinous consequences that are contrary to the very purpose of preventing crimes. The first is that it is far from easy to maintain the essential proportion between crime and punishment, for no matter how much industrious cruelty may have multiplied the forms of chastisement, they still cannot exceed the limit that the human physique and sensory capacity can endure.[5] Once this limit has been reached, it would not be possible to devise greater punishments for more harmful and atrocious crimes, and yet such punishments would be required to deter them. The second consequence is that impunity itself arises from the barbarity of punishments. There are limits to human capacities both for good and for evil, and a spectacle that is too brutal for humanity can only be a passing frenzy, never a permanent system such as the law must be. If the laws are indeed cruel, either they are changed or else fatal impunity results from the laws themselves.

Who would not tremble with horror when he reads in history books of the barbarous and useless torments that were devised and carried out in cold blood by men who were deemed wise? Who would not shudder to the depths of his being at the sight of thousands of poor wretches forced into a desperate return to the original state of nature by a misery that the law—which has always favored the few and trampled on the many—has either willed or permitted? Or at the spectacle of people accused of impossible crimes fabricated by timid ignorance? Or at the sight of persons whose only crime has been their fidelity to their own principles lacerated with deliberate formality and slow torture by men endowed with the same senses and hence with the same passions, providing a diverting show for a fanatical crowd?

XXVIII

THE DEATH PENALTY

This vain profusion of punishments, which has never made men better, has moved me to inquire whether capital punishment is truly useful and just in a well-organized state. By what alleged right can men slaughter their fellows? Certainly not by the authority from which sovereignty and law derive. That authority is nothing but the sum of tiny portions of the individual liberty of each person; it represents the general will, which is the aggregate of private wills. Who on earth has ever willed that other men should have the liberty to kill him? How could this minimal sacrifice of the liberty of each individual ever include the sacrifice of the greatest good of all, life itself?[1] And even if such were the case, how could this be reconciled with the principle that a man does not have the right to take his own life? And, not having this right himself, how could he transfer it to another person or to society as a whole?

The death penalty, then, is not a *right*—for I have shown that it cannot be so—but rather a war of the nation against a citizen, a campaign waged on the ground that the nation has judged the destruction of his being to be useful or necessary.[2] If I can demonstrate that capital punishment is neither useful nor necessary, however, I shall have vindicated the cause of humanity.

The death of a citizen cannot be deemed necessary except for two reasons. First, if he still has sufficient connections and such power that he can threaten the security of the nation even though he be deprived of his liberty, if his mere existence can produce a revolution dangerous to the established form of government, then his death is required. The death of such a citizen becomes necessary, then, when the nation is losing or recovering its liberty, or in times of anarchy, when disorder itself takes the place of law. Under the calm rule of law, however, and under a regime that has the full support of the nation, that is well armed against external and internal enemies with force and with public opinion (which is perhaps more effective than force itself), where only the true sovereign holds the power to command, and where riches buy pleasure and not authority, I see no necessity whatever for destroying a citizen.[3] The sole exception would be if his death were the one and only deterrent to dissuade others from committing crimes. This is the second reason for believing that capital punishment could be just and necessary.

48

If the experience of all ages, during which the ultimate punishment has never deterred men who were determined to harm society; if the example of the citizens of Rome; or if twenty years of the reign of the Empress Elizabeth of Muscovy, who has given the leaders of her people an illustrious example that is worth at least as much as many conquests bought with the blood of her country's sons[4]—if all this does not persuade men, who always suspect the voice of reason and heed the voice of authority, then one needs only to consult human nature in order to feel the truth of my assertion.

It is not the severity of punishment that has the greatest impact on the human mind, but rather its duration, for our sensibility is more easily and surely stimulated by tiny repeated impressions than by a strong but temporary movement. The rule of habit is universal over every sentient being, and, as man talks and walks and tends to his needs with the aid of habit, so moral ideas are fixed in his mind only by lasting and repeated blows. The most powerful restraint against crime is not the terrible but fleeting spectacle of a villain's death, but the faint and prolonged example of a man who, deprived of his liberty, has become a beast of burden, repaying the society he has offended with his labors. Each of us reflects, "I myself shall be reduced to such a condition of prolonged wretchedness if I commit similar misdeeds."[5] This thought is effective because it recurs quite frequently, and it is more powerful than the idea of death, which men always see in the hazy distance.

Capital punishment makes an impression which for all its force does not offset the rapid forgetfulness that is natural to man, even in the most essential matters, and that human passions accelerate. One may posit as a general rule that violent passions grip men strongly but not for long, and thus they are apt to cause those revolutions that turn ordinary men either into Persians or else into Spartans. Under a free and tranquil regime, however, impressions should be frequent rather than strong.

The death penalty becomes an entertainment for the majority and, for a few people, the object of pity mixed with scorn. Both of these sentiments alike fill the hearts of the spectators to a greater extent than does the salutary fear that the law claims to inspire. With moderate and continuous punishments, though, such fear is the dominant sentiment because it is the only one. The limit that the legislator should assign to the rigor of punishment, then, seems to be the point at which the feeling of compassion begins to outweigh every other emotion in the hearts of those who witness a chastisement that is really carried out for their benefit rather than for the sake of the criminal.[6]

/In order to be just, a penalty should have only the degree of intensity needed to deter other men from crime. Now there is no one who, on reflection, would choose the total and permanent loss of his own liberty, no matter how advantageous a crime might be. Therefore, the intensity of a sentence of servitude for life, substituted for the death penalty, has everything needed to deter the most determined spirit. Indeed, I would say more: a great many people look upon death with a tranquil and steady eye, some from fanaticism, others from vanity (a sentiment that almost always accompanies men even beyond the grave), some from a final and desperate attempt to live no longer or to leave their misery behind; but neither fanaticism nor vanity survives among fetters and chains, under the prod or the yoke, or in an iron cage, and the desperate man finds a beginning rather than an end to his troubles. Our spirit withstands violence and extreme yet fleeting pain better than it does time and unending weariness, for it can, so to speak, draw itself together for a moment to repel the former, but its elasticity is insufficient to resist the prolonged and repeated actions of the latter. With capital punishment, one crime is required for each example offered to the nation; with the penalty of a lifetime at hard labor, a single crime affords a host of lasting examples. Moreover, if it be important that men should see the power of the law frequently, judicial executions should not be separated by too great an interval; this presupposes frequent crimes. Thus, in order for this punishment to be useful, it must not make as strong an impression on men as it ought to make; in other words, it must be effective and ineffective at the same time. If someone were to say that life at hard labor is as painful as death and therefore equally cruel, I should reply that, taking all the unhappy moments of perpetual slavery together, it is perhaps even more painful, but these moments are spread out over a lifetime, and capital punishment exercises all its power in an instant. And this is the advantage of life at hard labor: it frightens the spectator more than the victim, for the former considers the entire sum of unhappy moments, and the latter is distracted from the future by the misery of the present moment. Imagination magnifies all evils, and the sufferer finds compensations and consolations unknown and unbelievable to the spectators, who substitute their own sensibility for the calloused soul of the wretch./

Here, more or less, is the line of reasoning that a thief or a murderer follows; such men have no motive but the gibbet or the wheel to keep them from breaking the law. (I am aware that developing the sentiments of one's spirit is an art that one acquires with education, but, though a thief would not express his principles well, they are no less operative for that.) "What are these laws that I must respect and that leave such a great distance between me and the rich man? He denies me the penny I ask of him, and he excuses himself by exhorting me to work, something with which he himself is unfamiliar. Who made these laws? Rich and powerful men who have never deigned to visit the squalid hovels of the poor, who have never broken a moldy crust of bread among the innocent cries of their famished children and the tears of their wives. Let us break these bonds that are so ruinous for the majority and useful to a handful of indolent tyrants; let us attack injustice at its source. I shall revert to my natural state of independence, and for a time I shall live free and happy from the fruits of my courage and industry. Perhaps I shall see the day of suffering and repentance, but that time will be brief, and, in return for a day of torment, I shall have many years of liberty and pleasure. King of a small band, I shall set fortune's errors right, and I shall see those tyrants grow pale and tremble in the presence of a man whom they, with insulting ostentation, respected less than their horses and dogs.''[7] Then religion appears to the mind of the scoundrel, who puts everything to bad use, and, presenting him with the prospect of an easy repentance and a near certainty of eternal bliss, greatly diminishes the horror of the final tragedy.

But the man who sees before his eyes the prospect of a great many years or even a lifetime of penal servitude and suffering, exposed to the sight of his fellow citizens with whom he once lived in freedom and friendship, a slave to the laws that once protected him, will make a salutary comparison between all this, on the one hand, and the uncertain success of his crimes and the brief time that he will be able to enjoy their fruits, on the other. The constant example of those whom he actually sees as victims of their own inadvertence makes a much stronger impression on him than the spectacle of a punishment that hardens more than it corrects him.

Capital punishment is not useful because of the example of cruelty which it gives to men. If the passions or the necessity of war have taught people to shed human blood, the laws that moderate men's conduct ought not to augment the cruel example, which is all the more pernicious because judicial execution is carried out methodically and formally. It appears absurd to me that the laws, which are the expression of the public will and which detest and punish homicide, commit murder themselves, and, in order to dissuade citizens from assassination, command public assassination. What are the true and most effective laws? They are those pacts and conventions that everyone would observe and propose while the voice of private interest, which one always hears, is silent or in agreement with the voice of the public interest.[8] What are the sentiments of each person regarding the death penalty? We may read them in the signs of indignation and scorn with which everyone looks upon the executioner, who is, however, an innocent servant of the public will, a

good citizen who contributes to the public welfare, the necessary instrument
of internal security just as valorous soldiers are of external security. What,
then, is the origin of this contradiction? And why is this sentiment that defies
reason indelible among men? Because men, in their heart of hearts, the part of
them that more than any other still retains the original form of their first
nature, have always believed that one's own life should be at the mercy only of
necessity, which rules the world with its iron scepter.

What must men think when they see wise magistrates and grave
ministers of justice who, with tranquil indifference and slow preparation, have
a criminal dragged to his death? And when they witness a judge who, with cold
insensitivity and perhaps even secret satisfaction in his own authority, goes to
enjoy the comforts and pleasures of life while a poor wretch writhes in his final
agony, awaiting the fatal blow? "Ah!" they will say, "these laws are only
pretexts for violence and for the premeditated and cruel formalities of justice;
they are only a conventional language for sacrificing us with greater security,
like victims offered up to the insatiable idol of despotism. We see assassination employed without repugnance or excitement, even though it is preached
to us as a horrible crime. Let us take advantage of this example. Violent death
appears a terrible sight as it is described to us, but we see that it is the affair of
a moment. How much less its terror will be for someone who, because he is not
expecting it, is spared almost all of its pain!" These are the pernicious and
fallacious arguments used more or less consciously by men disposed to crime.
Among such men, as we have seen, the abuse of religion carries more weight
than religion itself.

If anyone should cite against me the example of pratically all ages and
nations, which have assigned the death penalty to certain crimes, I shall reply
that the example is annihilated in the presence of truth, against which there is
no prescription, and that human history leaves us with the impression of a vast
sea of errors in which a few confused and widely scattered truths are floating.
Human sacrifice was common among virtually all nations, yet who will dare to
excuse it? That a mere handful of societies have abstained from capital
punishment for a short period only is more favorable than contrary to my case,
because this is similar to the fate of great truths. They last no longer than a
flash in comparison with the long dark night that surrounds humanity. The
happy period has not yet arrived in which truth shall be the portion of the majority, just as error has been hitherto. Until now, only those truths that Infinite
Wisdom has wished to distinguish by revealing them have been exempted
from this universal law. The voice of one philosopher is too weak to overcome
the hue and the cry of so many people who are guided by blind habit, but the

few sages scattered across the face of the earth will echo my sentiments in their inner-most hearts. And if Truth can reach the throne of a monarch despite the infinite obstacles that separate him from her and despite his own will, let him know that she comes with the secret desires of all men; let him know that the sanguinary notoriety of conquerors will fall silent before him and that a just posterity will give his name preeminence among the peaceful trophies of the Tituses, the Antonines, and the Trajans.[9]

How happy humanity would be if laws were being given to it for the first time, now that we see beneficent monarchs seated on the thrones of Europe! They are rulers who love peaceful virtue, the sciences and the arts; they are the fathers of their people, citizens who wear the crown. The growth of their authority consitutes the happiness of their subjects because it destroys that intermediary despotism, which is all the more cruel because it is less secure, that has stifled the expression of the desires of the people.[10] Those desires are always sincere and always fortunate when they can reach the throne. If such monarchs, I say, allow ancient laws to remain, it is the result of the infinite difficulty of stripping errors of the venerable rust of many centuries. This is a reason for enlightened citizens to desire more ardently the continued increase of their authority.[11]

XXIX

IMPRISONMENT

An error that is as common as it is contrary to the purpose of society (which is the awareness of one's personal security[1]) is the practice of allowing the magistrate who enforces the law the discretionary power to imprison a citizen, to deprive an enemy of his liberty upon frivolous pretexts, and to grant impunity to a friend in defiance of the strongest evidence of guilt.[2] Imprisonment is a punishment which differs from all others in that it must necessarily precede the verdict of guilt. This distinctive characteristic, however, does not deprive it of another one—namely, that only the law determines the cases in which a man deserves punishment. The law, therefore, shall specify what evidence of a crime requires the detention of the accused and makes him subject to interrogation and punishment. Public notoriety, flight, an extrajudicial confession, the confession of an accomplice, threats and constant enmity directed against the victim, the crime itself, and similar evidence are proofs sufficient to incarcerate a citizen; but these proofs must be established by law and not by judges, whose decrees are always contrary to political liberty unless they are particular applications of a general maxim in the public legal code. To the degree that punishments become moderate, that squalor and hunger are banished from prisons, and that compassion and humanity pass through the iron gates and take command of the inexorable and hardened ministers of justice, the law may be content with weaker and weaker evidence to imprison someone. A man accused of a crime, imprisoned, and acquitted, should not bear any trace of infamy. How many Romans accused of the most serious crimes and later found innocent were revered by the people and honored with public offices! Why, then, is the fate of an innocent person so different in our own day? Because it seems that with the current system of criminal jurisprudence, the idea of force and power carries more weight with public opinion than the idea of justice; because the accused and the convicted are thrown into the same cell indiscriminately; because incarceration is a punishment rather than a means for detaining the criminal; //and because the internal force that upholds the law is separate from the external force that defends the throne and the nation, though the two should be joined together. If they were, the internal force would be combined with the judiciary in a common dependence on the laws; it would not, however, derive its authority from the judiciary. The glory that accompanies the pomp and display of a military corps would remove infamy, which, like all feelings of the common crowd, is more attached to style than to substance, as is proved by the fact that, in common opinion, military imprisonment is less disgraceful than civilian incarceration.// Among the lower orders and their customs, and among laws (which are always more than a century behind the contemporary enlightened thought of a nation), there still remain the barbarous impressions and ferocious ideas of the northern huntsmen who were our ancestors.[3]

Some people have held that punishment may be assigned to a crime—that is, to an action contrary to the laws—no matter where it was committed; as though the status of being a subject were indelible, in other words, synonymous with, or even worse than, being a slave; as though someone could be a subject of one realm though a resident of another, and as though his acts could be under the jurisdiction of two sovereigns and two frequently conflicting law codes without contradiction. Some people likewise believe that a cruel act committed, for example, in Constantinople may be punished in Paris for the abstract reason that whoever offends humanity deserves the enmity of all mankind and universal execration; as though judges were the avengers of the sensibility of men in general rather than the vindicators of the contracts that bind men to one another. The place of punishment must be the place of the crime, for only there and not anywhere else are men compelled to take action against a private person in order to prevent a public offense. A man who is a scoundrel but who has not broken the contracts of a society of which he is not a member may be feared, and therefore the authorities of that society may exile and exclude him, but he may not be punished with legal formality. The law vindicates contracts, but it does not exact vengeance for the intrinsic malice of actions.

Ordinarily, persons who are guilty of lesser crimes are punished either by locking them in the darkness of a prison or by deporting them to nations that they have not offended, where, to serve as an example, they are subjected to a distant and therefore virtually useless servitude.[4] Since the decision to commit the worst crimes is not made on the spur of the moment, the public punishment of a major misdeed will be regarded by most people as something alien that could not happen to them, but the public punishment of lesser crimes, which are closer to their hearts, will dissuade them from minor infractions and deter them all the more from major ones. Punishments should be proportional to one another; they should also be proportional to the crime, not just in their severity, but in the manner in which they are carried out. Some persons escape punishment for a minor crime because the offended party forgives them. Such an act is in accordance with beneficence and humanity, but it is contrary to the public good; as though a private citizen by his pardon could remove the need to set an example in the same way that he can waive damages due for a civil offense. The right to inflict punishment does not belong to an individual, but to all citizens or to the sovereign. An individual can renounce only his own portion of this right; he cannot annul that of others.

XXX

PROCEEDINGS AND LIMITATIONS
ON CRIMINAL PROSECUTION

Once the evidence has been introduced and the certainty of the crime established, it is necessary to give the accused sufficient time and appropriate means to defend himself; but this time must be brief enough that it does not prejudice the promptness of punishment, which, as we have seen, is one of the principal restraints on crime. An ill-considered love of humanity seems to oppose such brevity, but every doubt will disappear if one considers that dangers to the innocent increase with legislative defects.

The law, however, should fix a certain period both for preparing the defense of the accused and for preparing the prosecution's case, and the judge would become a legislator if he were to determine the time necessary for preparing the evidence. Likewise, once really atrocious criminal cases that men remember for a long time have been proven, the perpetrator does not deserve the benefit of any delay in prosecution if he has saved himself by flight. But in minor and less notorious cases, there should be a statute of limitations relieving a citizen of uncertainty regarding his fate; for the long obscurity which has hidden his crimes makes the case insignificant as an example of impunity, and the criminal still has a chance to mend his ways. I confine myself to calling attention to these principles, for a precise limitation can be fixed only by specific legislation and in the given circumstances of a society. I shall add only that when a nation has recognized the usefulness of moderate punishments, then the laws that lengthen or shorten the period before immunity is granted or the time needed to prepare the evidence according to the seriousness of the crime, and that count the period of detention or voluntary exile as part of the sentence, will provide a simple classification consisting of a few mild punishments for a large number of crimes.

Such time limits, however, ought not to increase in exact proportion to the atrocity of the crime, for the likelihood of crimes is inversely proportional to their barbarity. Accordingly, the time allotted to judicial inquiry should sometimes be diminished and the delay in granting immunity against prosecution increased. This may appear to contradict what I have said, namely, that equal punishments may be assigned to unequal crimes, if the period of pretrial detention or of prescription before the sentence is taken into account. To explain my idea to the reader, I distinguish between two classes of crimes: the first is the category of atrocious crimes, beginning with murder and including all of the more extreme misdeeds; the second is the category of lesser offenses. This distinction is founded upon human nature. The security of one's own life is a natural right; the security of property is a social right.[1] The number of motives that move men to transgress the natural feeling of compassion is far less than the number of motives that, through the natural desire for happiness, move them to violate a right that they do not find in their hearts but in the conventions of society. The great difference in probability between these two classes of crimes requires that the two categories be governed by different principles. Since the most terrible crimes are the least common, the period of judicial examination should decrease in view of the greater likelihood of the innocence of the accused. The time before immunity is granted, however, should be lengthened, because only a definite verdict of guilt or innocence can remove the enticing hope of impunity, and the harmful effects of impunity grow with the seriousness of the crime. But with minor crimes, given the lesser likelihood of the innocence of the accused, the period of judicial investigation should be extended, and, as the pernicious consequences of impunity decline, the delay in granting immunity from further prosecution should be shortened. Such a division of crimes into two classes would be inadmissible if the harm of letting offenses go unpunished were to decrease in exact proportion to the increasing probability of the crime. /One should keep in mind that an accused person whose guilt or innocence has not been established, even though he may be at large for lack of evidence, can be subjected anew to arrest and examination for the same crime if new evidence of the sort the law requires comes to light, provided that the time fixed by the statute of limitations pertaining to his crime has not expired. This, at any rate, seems to me the most suitable arrangement for defending both the security and the liberty of the subject, for it is all too easy to favor one at the expense of the other. Thus these two blessings that constitute the inalienable and equal birthright of every citizen are in danger of being left unprotected and uncared for, the one against open or concealed despotism, the other against turbulent mob anarchy./

XXXI

CRIMES
DIFFICULT TO PROVE

In view of these principles, it will appear strange to anyone who fails to consider that reason has almost never been the lawgiver of nations that the most atrocious or the most obscure of crimes—in other words, those that are most unlikely—are the ones proved by conjecture and by the weakest and most equivocal evidence; as though the law and the judge were not interested in seeking the truth, but in establishing the fact of a crime; as though the danger of condemning an innocent man were not all the greater as the probability of his innocence surpasses the likelihood of his guilt. Most men lack that vigor which is equally necessary for great crimes and great virtues; thus, it seems that the former always coexist with the latter in those nations that sustain themselves by the activity of their governments and by passions working together for the public good, rather than in countries that depend on their size or the invariable excellence of their laws. In the latter sort of nation, weakened passions seem better suited to the maintenance rather than to the improvement of the form of government. From this, one can draw an important conclusion: that great crimes in a nation are not always a proof of its decline.

There are some crimes that are both frequent in society and difficult to prove, and, in such cases, the difficulty of establishing guilt takes the place of the probability of innocence. In cases of this nature, the danger arising from impunity is less significant, because the frequency with which the crimes occur has no relationship to escaping punishment. Therefore, the time allotted for judicial inquiry and the statutory delay in granting immunity against prosecution should both be curtailed. Yet adultery and pederasty, which are crimes difficult to prove, are the ones that, according to accepted principles, admit of tyrannical presumptions, of *quasi-proofs* and *semi-proofs* (as if a man could be *semi-innocent* or *half-guilty*, which is to say, *semi-punishable* and *half-acquittable*)¹; these are the crimes, too, in which torture exercises its cruel sway over the person of the accused, over the witnesses, and even over the whole family of a poor wretch, according to the coldly iniquitous teaching of certain learned men who set themselves up as the rule and precept for judges.

Adultery is a crime that, politically considered, derives its strength and

58

orientation from two causes: variable human laws and that very strong attraction which impels one sex toward the other. The latter is similar in many respects to the force of gravity which moves the universe; for, like gravity, it diminishes with distance, and, if the one influences all the movements of bodies, so the other, throughout its duration, influences almost all movements of the spirit. The two differ in this, that gravity reaches a state of equilibrium with obstructions, while sexual attraction generally gathers strength and vigor with the growth of the very obstacles opposed to it.[2]

If I were to speak to nations still deprived of the light of religion, I would say that there is yet another considerable difference between adultery and other crimes. Adultery arises from the abuse of a need that is constant and universal throughout the human race, a need that is anterior to society and, indeed, on which society itself was founded, whereas other crimes tending to the destruction of society originate more from the promptings of momentary passion than from natural need. For someone who knows history and human nature, the intensity of such a need always appears to be constant in a given climate. If such is the case, laws and customs that seek to diminish the total sum would be useless and even pernicious, for the effect would be to burden some peoples with the needs of others in addition to their own.[3] On the contrary, truly wise laws and customs, following the gentle slope of the plain, as it were, would divide and distribute the total river into a number of equal portions sufficient to prevent both drought and flooding everywhere. Conjugal fidelity always depends on the number and freedom of marriages. Where hereditary prejudices hold sway over marriages, where such unions are arranged or broken by familial authority, secret love affairs undo their bonds in spite of common morality, whose business is to inveigh against the effects while condoning the causes.[4] Such reflections, however, are useless for someone who, imbued with true religion, has more sublime motives that correct the force of natural impulses. A crime of this sort is an act so quickly committed and so mysterious, so covered by the very veil with which the law has shrouded it (a necessary veil, but one so delicate as to increase rather than diminish the desirability of what it covers), the opportunities for it are so easy, and the consequences are so equivocal, that the legislator will find it easier to prevent rather than correct this offense. As a general rule, with every crime which, because of its very nature, goes unpunished most of the time, the punishment becomes an incentive. It is characteristic of our imagination that difficulties, if they are not insurmountable or too great for the mental laziness of particular persons, excite the imagination more vividly and magnify the object of our desires. Difficulties are like so many barriers that prevent our errant and fickle imagination from deserting that particular object. Constrained to examine every aspect, our imagination fastens more securely on the pleasant part, toward which our mind is drawn quite naturally, whereas it flees and withdraws from the painful and harmful.

Pederasty, so severely punished by the laws and so easily subjected to the torments that conquer innocence, is founded less upon the needs of the isolated and free man than upon the passions of the sociable and enslaved man.[5] It draws its strength not so much from a surfeit of pleasures as from the sort of education that begins by making men useless to themselves in order to make them useful to others. It is the result of those institutions where hot-blooded youth is confined and where there is an insurmountable barrier to every other sort of relationship; all developing natural vigor is wasted in a way that is useless to humanity and that brings on premature old age.[6]

Infanticide is likewise the effect of an inevitable contradiction, one in which a woman is placed when she has either submitted out of weakness or been overpowered by violence. Faced with a choice between disgrace and the death of a creature incapable of feeling pain, who would not prefer the latter to the unavoidable misery to which the woman and her unfortunate offspring would be exposed? The best way to prevent this crime would be to protect weakness with effective laws against tyranny, which exaggerates those vices that cannot be covered with the cloak of virtue.[7]

I do not pretend to diminish the just horror which these crimes deserve. Having called attention to their origins, however, I believe that I am entitled to draw a general conclusion: namely, that a punishment for a crime cannot be deemed truly just (which is to say, necessary) unless the laws have adopted the best possible means, in the given circumstances of a nation, to prevent that crime.

XXXII

SUICIDE[1]

Suicide is a crime that seems not to admit of a punishment properly speaking, for punishment could only fall upon the innocent or upon a cold and insensible corpse. If the latter will make no more impression on the living than whipping a statue would, the former is unjust and tyrannical, for men's political liberty necessarily demands that punishments be entirely personal.[2] Men love life too much, and everything surrounding them confirms them in this love. The seductive image of pleasure, and hope, the sweetest illusion of mortals, which leads us to swallow great draughts of evil mixed with a few drops of contentment, are too alluring for anyone to fear that the necessary impunity of such a crime should have much influence on men. Whoever fears pain obeys the law, but death extinguishes all sources of bodily pain. What motive, then, will restrain the suicide's desperate hand?

Whoever kills himself does less damage to society than someone who leaves its boundaries forever, for the former leaves all of his substance behind, whereas the latter removes himself and a part of his possessions. Indeed, if the strength of a society lies in the number of its citizens, the expatriate, by withdrawing himself and joining a neighboring nation, does twice the harm of the suicide, who simply removes himself from society with his death. The issue, then, comes down to knowing whether it is useful or harmful to a nation to allow each of its members a perpetual freedom to live elsewhere.[3]

Any law that has no force behind it or that circumstances render ineffectual ought not to be promulgated. Further, just as opinion, the ruler of men's minds, obeys legislative influence when it is slow and roundabout and resists that influence when it is direct and violent, so useless laws that men scorn infect even the most salutary laws with their baseness; then, even good laws are seen as an obstacle to be overcome rather than as the depository of the public welfare. Indeed, if, as has been said, our capacity for feeling is limited, the more veneration men have for objects foreign to the law, so much the less will remain for the law itself. From this principle the wise administrator of the public happiness can draw several useful consequences that, were I to elaborate, would take me too far away from my subject, which is to prove how useless it is to turn the state into a prison. A law to this effect is useless. Unless a country be cut off from every other by inaccessible cliffs or unnavigable seas, how can every point of its boundaries be closed? And who will guard the guards? A man who flees the country with all his possessions cannot be punished precisely because he has done so. As soon as it is committed, a crime of this sort cannot be punished, and to punish it beforehand is to penalize men's wills and not their actions; it amounts to commanding a man's intention, which is the part of him that is freest from the sway of human law. //To punish the expatriate by seizing the property he has left—which, quite apart from the ease and inevitability of collusion, could not be accomplished without tyrannizing over contracts—would stifle all commerce between one nation and another.// Punishing the criminal when he returns would be to prevent the harm done to society from being repaired by making all absences permanent. The very prohibition against leaving a country heightens the desire of its citizens to leave and serves as a warning to foreigners not to enter.

What must we think of a government that has no means except fear to keep men in the country to which they are bound by their earliest childhood impressions? The surest way of attaching citizens to their fatherland is to improve the relative well-being of each of them. Just as every effort ought to be made to turn the balance of trade in our favor,[4] so it is in the greatest interest of the sovereign and of the nation that the sum total of happiness compared with that of neighboring nations should be greater than elsewhere. The pleasures of luxury are not the chief elements of this happiness, although they are a necessary remedy for inequality, which always grows with the progress of a nation. Without these pleasures, all wealth would become concentrated in one set of hands.[5] Where the borders of a nation are expanding at a faster rate than its population, luxury favors despotism, //in part because where men are more scarce, industry is accordingly less, and the less industry there is, the more the poor depend on the ostentation of the rich. At the same time, it is all the more difficult for the poor to unite against their oppressors, and it is less to be feared. Another reason is that the homage, public offices, distinctions, and submission that make people aware of the distance between the strong and the weak are more easily obtained from few than from many, for men are more independent when they are less observed, and they are less observed the greater their numbers are.// Where population is increasing at a greater rate than territory, on the other hand, luxury is opposed to despotism because it stimulates men's industry and activity. The needs of the poor, moreover, offer the rich too many pleasures and comforts to leave much room for those of pure ostentation, which strengthen feelings of dependence. Thus, we may observe that in vast, weak, and underpopulated states, luxury of ostentation is more prevalent than luxury of pleasure, if nothing else stands in the way; but in states that are large in population rather than territory, luxury of comfort diminishes this luxury of ostentation.[6] The commerce and exchange of pleasures, however, have this disadvantage, that, although many people are involved, this sort of trade still begins and ends with a few people, and the majority of the population enjoys only a tiny share. That share is insufficient to check feelings of want, which arise more from comparison than from reality.[7] But the true foundations of the happiness I mentioned are security and freedom limited only by law. Accompanied by these, the pleasures of luxury favor the common people, and, without them, such pleasures become the instrument of tyranny. Just as the noblest beasts and the freest birds withdraw to wastes and inaccessible forests and abandon the fertile and smiling plains to man with his snares, so men flee from pleasures themselves when the hand of tyranny offers them.

Thus it is demonstrated that a law which imprisons subjects in their country is useless and unjust. Therefore, it is likewise useless and unjust to punish suicide, and, on that account, although it is a crime which God punishes (since He alone can punish even after death), it is not a crime before men, since the punishment, instead of falling on the criminal himself, falls on his family. If anyone objects by telling me that such a penalty can nonetheless deter a man bent on killing himself, my reply is that someone who calmly renounces the advantages of life, who detests his existence here below to the point of preferring an eternity of unhappiness, is not at all likely to be moved by the less effective and more distant consideration of his children and relatives.

XXXIII

SMUGGLING[1]

Smuggling is truly a crime that offends the sovereign and the nation, but its punishment should not entail disgrace, since public opinion does not deem this act disgraceful. Anyone who assigns shameful punishments to crimes that are not reputed to be shameful among men destroys the feeling of infamy for crimes that really are infamous. Whoever sees the same death penalty applied, for example, to someone who kills a pheasant and to someone who assassinates a man or who forges an important document, will not make any distinction among these crimes. This destroys moral sentiments, which are the work of many centuries and of much bloodshed and which have been produced in the human spirit very slowly and with difficulty; their birth was thought to require the support of the most sublime motives and an enormous apparatus of solemn formal observances.

This crime arises from the law itself, since its advantages always grow with the tariff, and hence the temptation to smuggle and the ease of doing so increase with the boundaries to be guarded and with the reduction in the volume of merchandise itself.[2] The penalty of losing both the contraband merchandise and the goods that accompany it is quite just, but it will be more effective to the degree that the customs duty is smaller, since men take risks only in proportion to the success that their uncertain enterprise might yield.

But why does this crime not bring disgrace upon its perpetrators, since it is a theft committed against the prince and, consequently, against the nation itself? My answer is that offenses that men do not believe could be done to them do not interest them enough to arouse public indignation against the perpetrators. Men, upon whom remote consequences make a very weak impression, do not see the harm smuggling can do them. Indeed, they often enjoy its immediate advantages. They see only the harm it does to the prince, and therefore they do not see as much reason to disapprove of a smuggler as they do to detest someone who robs a private person, forges a document, or commits some other crime that might harm them personally. It is an obvious principle that every sentient being is concerned only with those evils with which he is acquainted.

But should such a crime go unpunished when it is committed by someone who has no possessions to forfeit? No. Some types of smuggling so affect public revenue (which is such an essential and such a difficult part of a good system of legislation) that this sort of offense deserves a considerable penalty, to the extent even of prison or penal servitude—though imprisonment and servitude should fit the nature of the crime itself. For example, the prison sentence of a tobacco smuggler should not be the same as that of a cutthroat or a thief, and the smuggler's labor, if confined to the work and service of the royal revenue adminstration that he had meant to defraud, will be the most suitable type of punishment.

XXXIV

DEBTORS

The good faith of contracts and the security of commerce oblige the legislator to take custody of the persons of insolvent debtors on behalf of their creditors. I believe it is important, however, to distinguish the fraudulent from the innocent bankrupt. The former should be punished with the same penalty assigned to counterfeiters, because counterfeiting a piece of coined metal, which is a pledge of obligation among citizens, is no greater crime than counterfeiting the obligations themselves. //But the innocent bankrupt, the person who has proved before his judges after a rigorous examination that he has been stripped of his substance, either by the malice or misfortune of others or by vicissitudes that human prudence cannot avoid—upon what barbarous pretext can he be thrown into prison where, deprived of his one poor remaining possession, bare liberty, he experiences the agonies of the guilty and, with the desperation of downtrodden honesty, he perhaps repents of the innocence that permitted him to live peacefully under the tutelage of the laws he broke through no fault of his own? Such laws are dictated by the powerful out of greed and endured by the weak for the sake of that hope which usually shines in the human heart, making us believe that adversity is for others and good fortune for ourselves. The natural tendency of men is to love cruel laws, even though moderate ones would better suit their interest, since they themselves are subject to these laws; the fear of being injured, however, is greater than the desire to do harm. Let us return to the innocent bankrupt. I admit that his obligations should not be cancelled until they have been paid in full, that he should not be allowed to escape them without the consent of the interested parties, and that he should not be allowed to remove his business to another jurisdiction. Under penalty, he should be compelled to conduct his business so as to give satisfaction to his creditors in proportion to his earnings. What legitimate pretext, then, such as the security of commerce or the sacred right of property, could justify depriving an innocent bankrupt of his freedom? This would be useless, except in an instance when the evils of penal servitude might bring the secrets of an allegedly innocent bankrupt to light—a rare case indeed if there has been a rigorous investigation! I believe it a maxim of legislation that the importance of the political disadvantages that follow from these principles is directly proportional to the immediate damage done to society and inversely proportional to the difficulty of verifying that damage. One should be able to distinguish fraud from a serious fault, a serious fault from a slight one, and the latter from complete innocence. Assigning to the first sort of criminal, the one guilty of fraud, penalties for crimes of forgery; meting out lesser punishments, though still including loss of liberty to the second; and reserving for the last, the innocent, a free choice of the means of restitution, one should deprive the third sort of criminal, the one who has committed a slight fault, of such a choice, leaving it to his creditors instead. The distinction between serious and slight faults, however, should be fixed by blind and impartial laws, not by the dangerous and arbitrary discretion of judges. Establishing limits is as important in politics as in mathematics, in measuring the public good as in measuring size.*

How easy it would be for a farsighted legislator to prevent much fraudulent bankruptcy and to relieve the misfortunes of the innocent and the industrious! Public and open registration of all contracts, coupled with freedom for all citizens to consult these well-ordered documents; a public bank funded by taxes wisely levied on prosperous trade and designed to provide timely financial assistance to unfortunate but innocent businessmen—these measures would have no real drawbacks, and they could produce innumerable advantages. Easy, simple, and great laws, however, laws that require only a nod from the legislator to spread wealth and vigor throughout the nation, laws that would receive hymns of undying gratitude from generation to generation—such laws are the ones least thought of or least desired. A restless and carping spirit, a timid prudence that sees only the present moment, and a wary rigidity against any innovation dominate the feelings of those who control the bustling activity of petty mortals.[2]//

//*Commerce and the ownership of goods are not the goal of the social contract, but they can be a means of achieving it. To expose all the members of society to the evils which are the reason that society has formed so many arrangements would be to subordinate the ends to the means. This is a fallacious proceeding in all the sciences and especially in the science of politics; it is one into which I fell in earlier editions of this book, where I said that the innocent bankrupt should be kept in custody as a pledge of his debts or made to work as a slave for his creditors. I am ashamed of having written this way. I have been accused of irreligion, and I did not deserve it. I have been accused of sedition, and I did not deserve it.[1] I have offended the rights of humanity, and yet no one has reproached me for it!//

XXXV

PLACES

OF ASYLUM

There remain two questions for me to examine. The first is whether places of asylum are just and whether treaties among nations for the reciprocal extradition of criminals are useful or not. Within the borders of a country, there should be no place independent of its laws. Their power should follow every citizen as a shadow follows a body. There is only a difference of degree between impunity and asylum, and, just as the impression that punishment makes owes more to the certainty of receiving it than to its severity, so places of asylum encourage crime more than punishments deter it. To multiply places of asylum is to create so many small sovereign entities, for where the laws do not hold authority, there new laws differing from the common law may be made; hence a spirit opposed to the spirit of the whole body of society may arise.[1] All history shows that great revolutions in states and in human opinions come out of places of asylum. But is it useful for nations to extradite one another's criminals? I shall not venture to decide this question until laws more in harmony with human needs, more moderate punishments, and the extinction of dependence on whim and opinion have established the security of innocence and downtrodden virtue; until universal reason, which always draws the interests of the throne and of subjects closer together, has confined tyranny entirely to the vast plains of Asia. The belief that there is no plot of ground where true crimes go unpunished, however, would be a most effective means of preventing them.

XXXVI

BOUNTIES

The other question is whether it is useful to put a price on the head of a known criminal, thereby arming the hand of each citizen and making him an executioner. Either the criminal is outside the country or he is within its boundaries. In the first case, the sovereign incites his citizens to commit a crime and expose themselves to punishment, thereby injuring other realms and usurping their authority and authorizing them in this way to do the same to himself. If the criminal is still in the country, the sovereign displays his own weakness by offering a bounty; whoever has the power to defend himself does not seek to buy it. Further, such an edict overthrows all ideas of morality and virtue, which are apt to vanish from the human spirit at the slightest breeze. At one moment the laws encourage treachery; at another, they punish it. With one hand the legislator strengthens the bonds of family, kindred, and friendship, and with the other he rewards those who violate and despise them. Always contradicting himself, at one instant he calls upon suspicious human minds to be trusting, and at the next he spreads distrust in every heart. Instead of preventing crimes, he instigates a hundred. These are the expedients of weak nations whose laws are but hasty repairs to a building that is in ruins with every portion crumbling. To the extent that a nation grows more enlightened, good faith and mutual confidence become necessary, and these tend to identify themselves more and more with sound policy. Trickery, intrigues, and dark and devious ways are foreseen for the most part, and the sensibility of everyone checks the sensibility of each particular individual. Even the centuries of ignorance, in which public morality compelled men to obey private standards, serve as instruction and experience for enlightened ages.[1] Laws that reward betrayal, stir up a clandestine war, and sow mutual suspicion among citizens, however, are opposed to that very necessary union of morality and public policy that would bring happiness to men, peace to nations, and, to the world, a somewhat longer period of tranquillity and respite from the evils that trample upon it.

XXXVII

/ATTEMPTED CRIMES,
ACCOMPLICES, AND IMPUNITY

Although the law does not punish intention, it by no means follows that an act which is the beginning of a crime and which clearly shows the will to carry it through does not deserve punishment, though a lesser one than for the actual execution of the crime. The importance of preventing a criminal attempt justifies a penalty, but, as there may be an interval between the initial undertaking and the completion of a crime, reserving the greater punishment for the crime that has been carried out may lead to repentance. One may say as much (though for other reasons) when there are several accomplices in a crime not all of whom are its direct perpetrators. When several men join in a risky undertaking, the greater the risk is, the more they try to divide it equally among them; thus it will be more difficult for them to find one of their number who will take upon himself alone the actual execution of the criminal act, thereby running a greater risk than the other accomplices. The one exception would be the case in which the perpetrator was assigned a certain reward; as he would then have compensation for his greater risk, the punishment fixed for him and his associates should be the same. Such reflections may seem too theoretical and refined to those who do not consider that it is most useful for the law to provide the fewest possible grounds for agreement among partners in crime.

Some tribunals offer impunity to an accomplice in a serious crime who will turn in his companions. Such an expedient has its drawbacks and its advantages. The disadvantages are that the nation authorizes betrayal, which is detestable even among scoundrels. Further, crimes of courage are less fatal to a nation than cowardly crimes, for courage is not common, and it needs only a benevolent guiding hand to make it work for the public good. Cowardice, however, is more common and contagious, and it is always more self-centered and self-sustaining. Again, the court shows its own uncertainty and the weakness of the law by imploring the aid of those who break it. The advantages of offering immunity from prosecution are that it prevents serious offenses and that it reassures the people, who are frightened by crimes whose effects are apparent and whose perpetrators are unknown. Moreover, it helps to show that a person who breaks faith with the laws (which is to say, with public conventions) will probably not keep faith in his private dealings. It would seem to me that a general statute promising impunity to an accomplice who gives information about any crime whatever would be preferable to a special declaration in a particular case, for the mutual fear of taking a risk by himself that each accomplice would have would prevent association in crime. The court would not encourage the audacity of criminals by letting them see that their help was needed in a specific instance. Such a law, however, should couple impunity for the informer with banishment— But in vain I torment myself to overcome the remorse I feel for authorizing the inviolable laws—the monument of public trust, the foundation of human morality—to suborn betrayal and dissimulation. What an example it would be to the nation, then, if they failed to grant the promised immunity from prosecution; if, by means of learned quibbles, someone who had accepted the invitation of the laws were dragged to punishment in spite of public pledges! Instances of this sort are not rare among nations, and hence there is no lack of people who see in a nation only a complicated mechanism whose parts are moved at will by those who are most clever and powerful. Cold and insensible to all that constitutes the delight of tender and sublime spirits, such men with imperturbable sagacity excite the most tender feelings or the most violent passions as they require, playing upon men's souls as musicians do upon their instruments.[1]

XXXVIII

SUGGESTIVE INTERROGATIONS
AND DEPOSITIONS

Our laws prohibit so-called *suggestive* lines of questioning in a trial, in other words, lines of questioning that, according to learned jurists, bear upon what is *special* about the circumstances of a crime, not upon what is *general* as they ought to do. Such interrogations, as they have a direct connection with the crime, *suggest* to the accused an immediate answer. Lines of questioning, according to specialists in criminal law, ought never to go straight to the fact, but should surround it, so to speak, as if with a spiral. The reason for proceeding this way is either so as not to *suggest* to the accused an answer that faces him squarely with the charge, or perhaps because it seems contrary to nature for a suspect to be his own direct accuser. For whichever of the two reasons it may be, it is a remarkable contradiction in the laws that they authorize torture along with this concern, yet what sort of interrogation could be more *suggestive* than pain? The first reason applies to torture, because pain will *suggest* to a robust fellow an obstinate silence by which he can exchange a greater for a lesser punishment; to a weakling, pain will *suggest* confession by which he can free himself from his present torment that, for the time being, has a greater effect on him than future pain. The second reason evidently applies to torture as well, for if a *special* line of questioning makes a criminal confess despite his natural right, agony will make him do so much more easily. Men, however, are guided more by differences in the names of things than by differences in the things themselves. Noteworthy among other abuses of language (which have no small influence on human affairs[1]) is the one that renders null and void the testimony of a criminal who has already been condemned. He is *dead in law,* the sage masters of jurisprudence gravely declare, and someone who is *dead* is incapable of any action. To support this empty metaphor, many victims have been sacrificed, and it has often been argued in all seriousness whether truth should yield to judicial formulas. Provided that the testimony of a condemned criminal is not such that it obstructs the course of justice, why, even after sentence has been passed, in consideration of the criminal's extreme misery and in the interest of truth, should he not be allowed a period to present new evidence sufficient to alter the nature of the case, so that he may be able to clear himself or others in a new trial? Formalities and ceremonies are necessary in the administration of justice, whether in order to leave nothing to the arbitrary discretion of the administrators, or in order to give the common people the idea of a judgment that is stable and orderly rather than violent and partisan, or because men are creatures and slaves of habit and are more affected by sense impressions than by rational arguments. But the law cannot, without grave danger, establish formalities and ceremonies in such a way as to harm the truth. Either because it is too simple or too complicated, truth needs some sort of external show to win over the ignorant populace. Finally, someone who obstinately refuses to answer the questions put to him deserves one of the most severe sorts of punishment established by law, so that men may not in that way evade their obligation to the public to furnish an example. Punishment in such an instance is not necessary when it is beyond all doubt that a certain man has committed a particular crime, for in that case interrogation is useless, just as a confession is when other proofs establish guilt. This last sort of case is the most common, for experience shows that in most trials the accused plead not guilty./

XXXIX

A PARTICULAR
KIND OF CRIME

The reader of this work will notice that I have omitted a kind of crime which covered Europe with human blood and raised those terrible pyres where living human bodies fed the fire. It was a pleasing entertainment and an agreeable concert of the blind mob to hear the muffled, confused groans of poor wretches issuing out of vortices of black smoke—the smoke of human limbs— amid the crackling of charred bones and the sizzling of still palpitating entrails. But rational men will see that the place where I live, the present age, and the matter at hand do not permit me to examine the nature of such a crime. It would take me too long and too far from my subject to prove how a perfect uniformity of thought is necessary in a state, the example of many nations to the contrary notwithstanding; how opinions that differ only on a few subtle and obscure points altogether beyond human comprehension can nonetheless disturb public order if one of them is not authorized to the exclusion of the others; and how opinions are so constituted that, while some are made clear by mutual fermentation and conflict, so that true ideas rise to the top and false ones sink into oblivion, the mere substance of other opinions is uncertain, and these need to be vested with authority and power.[1] It would take me too long to prove that, however odious the triumph of force over human minds may seem, since the only fruits of its conquest are dissembling and, consequently, degradation; however contrary it may seem to the spirit of gentleness and brotherly love enjoined by reason and the authority we most revere; it is still necessary and indispensable. All of this must be regarded as clearly demonstrated and in the best interest of mankind, provided that it is exercised by someone with acknowledged authority.[2] I speak only of crimes that arise from human nature and from the social contract. I do not address myself to sins; their punishment, even in this world, should be governed by principles other than those of a narrow philosophy.[3]

XL

FALSE IDEAS
OF UTILITY

One source of errors and injustices is the false ideas of utility at which legislators arrive. It is a false idea of utility to set particular inconveniences ahead of general inconveniences, to command feelings rather than to excite them, to command logical thought to obey. It is a false idea of utility to sacrifice a thousand real advantages for the sake of one disadvantage which is either imaginary or of little consequence; this would take fire away from men because it burns and water because it drowns people; this is to have no remedy for evils except destruction.[1] //Laws forbidding people to bear arms are of this nature; they only disarm those who are neither inclined nor determined to commit crimes. On the other hand, how can someone who has the courage to violate the most sacred laws of humanity and the most important ones in the statute books be expected to respect the most trifling and purely arbitrary regulations that can be broken with ease and impunity and that, were they enforced, would put an end to personal liberty—so dear to each man, so dear to the enlightened legislator—and subject the innocent to all the vexations that the guilty deserve? Such laws place the assaulted at a disadvantage and the assailant at an advantage, and they multiply rather than decrease the number of murders, since an unarmed person may be attacked with greater confidence than someone who is armed. These laws should not be deemed preventive, but rather inspired by a fear of crime. They originate with the tumultuous impact of a few isolated facts, not with a rational consideration of the drawbacks and the advantages of a universal decree.// It is a false idea of utility to wish to impose upon a multitude of sentient beings the symmetry and order that is the lot of brute, inanimate matter; to neglect present motives, which alone act with constancy and firmness upon the common crowd, in favor of remote influences, which make only an extremely transitory and weak impression, unless an extraordinary power of imagination magnifies them, making up for their remoteness.[2] Finally, it is a false idea of utility to sacrifice things to names by separating the public good from the good of all individuals.[3] There is this difference betwen the social state and the state of nature: the savage does no more harm to others than is necessary to do good to himself, but the sociable man is sometimes moved by bad laws to injure others without doing himself any good.[1] The despot sows fear and dejection in the hearts of his slaves, but these evils rebound and return with greater force to torment his own heart. The more private and domestic fear is, the less dangerous it is to the man who makes it the instrument of his happiness; the more public it is, however, and the more it affects a large number of people, the easier it becomes for someone who is careless or desperate or audaciously clever to make others serve his purposes, inspiring in them feelings that are all the more welcome and seductive as the risk of the undertaking is spread over a greater number of people.[5] Besides, the value that unhappy creatures set on their own lives diminishes in proportion to the misery they suffer. This is the reason why wrongs breed new wrongs: hatred is a more lasting sentiment than love, inasmuch as hatred draws its strength from continuous activity, which weakens love.

XLI

HOW TO PREVENT CRIMES

It is better to prevent crimes than to punish them. This is the chief purpose of every good system of legislation, which is the art of leading men to the greatest possible happiness, or rather, to speak in accordance with all reckonings of the blessings and evils of life, to the least possible unhappiness.[1] But the means hitherto employed for this purpose have been completely mistaken and contrary to the proposed aim. It is not possible to reduce turbulent human activity to a geometric order devoid of irregularity and confusion. Just as the constant and very simple laws of nature do not prevent perturbations in the movement of the planets, so human laws cannot prevent disturbances and disorders amid the infinite and utterly conflicting attractions of pleasure and pain. This, nonetheless, is the chimera of narrow-minded men when they hold power. To prohibit a host of harmless acts is not to prevent the crimes to which they might lead; it is, rather, to create new crimes; it is to define virtue and vice (which are preached to us as eternal and immutable) at one's whim. To what a state we should be reduced if everything that might tempt us to crime were forbidden to us! This would require that man be deprived of the use of his senses. For every motive that moves men to commit one real crime, there are a thousand that move them to commit those harmless acts which bad laws call crimes. Further, if the likelihood of crimes is proportional to the number of motives, to extend the sphere of acts deemed criminal is to increase the probability that they will be committed. The majority of laws are only privileges, which is to say, a tribute by all to the convenience of a few.

Do you want to prevent crimes? See to it that the laws are clear and simple, that the entire strength of the nation is concentrated in their defense, and that no portion of that strength is employed in their destruction.[2] /See to it that the law favors classes of men less than it favors men themselves./ See to it that men fear the laws and only the laws. The fear of the laws is salutary, but the fear of one man for another is a fertile source of crimes. Enslaved men are more sensual, more debauched, and more cruel than free men. The latter think about the sciences; they think about the interests of the nation; they see great examples, and they imitate them. The former, on the other hand, content with the present moment, seek a distraction for the emptiness of their lives in the tumult of debauchery. Accustomed to uncertain results in everything, the doubts they have about the outcome of their crimes strengthens the passions by which crimes are determined. If uncertainty about the laws befalls a nation made indolent by its climate, it supports and intensifies that nation's apathy and stupidity.[3] If such uncertainty befalls a sensual but active nation, the upshot is a dispersal of energy in an infinite number of petty plots and intrigues that sow distrust in every heart and make betrayal and dissembling the foundation of prudence. If it befalls a courageous and strong nation, the uncertainty is finally removed, but only after causing many fluctuations from liberty to slavery and from slavery to liberty.

XLII

KNOWLEDGE

Do you want to prevent crimes? See to it that enlightenment accompanies liberty. The evils that come from knowledge decline with its diffusion, and the benefits increase. An audacious imposter (who is always a more than ordinary man) wins the admiration of an ignorant people and the hisses of an enlightened one. By facilitating comparisons and multiplying points of view, knowledge opposes one sentiment to another and causes them to modify each other; this is all the more easily accomplished when one perceives that others have the same views and the same dislikes. In the face of widespread enlightenment in a nation, slanderous ignorance falls silent, and all authority not justified by sound reasons trembles. The vigorous force of the law, however, remains unshaken, for there is no enlightened man who does not love the open, clear, and useful contracts of public security when he compares the slight portion of useless liberty that he has sacrificed to the total sum of all the liberty sacrificed by other men. Without the restraints of law, that liberty might have been turned against him. Anyone who has a sensitive spirit, glancing at a well-made law code and finding that he has lost only the pernicious freedom to harm others, cannot but bless the throne and its occupant.

It is not true that learning has always been injurious to humanity, and, when it was, it was an unavoidable evil for men.[1] The multiplication of the human race upon the face of the earth introduced war, the cruder arts, and the first laws, which were temporary pacts born of necessity and dying with it. This was the first philosophy of men, and its few elements were just, since men's apathy and their small fund of sagacity preserved them from error. But needs increased more and more as men multiplied. Stronger and more lasting impressions, therefore, were necessary to prevent them from returning repeatedly to their original and increasingly ruinous unsociable condition. These primitive errors, then, that populated the earth with false deities and created an invisible universe which governs our own, were a great benefit for humanity—I mean a great political benefit. Those who dared to deceive men and lead the ignorant and docile crowd to altars were benefactors of mankind. By presenting people with objectives beyond the grasp of the senses, objectives which escaped them as soon as they believed them to be within reach,

76

things which were never despised because they were never well understood, these beneficent impostors united men's divided passions and concentrated them upon a single object that absorbed their attention entirely. These were the first events experienced by all nations that were molded from savage hordes. This was the epoch of the formation of great societies, and such was the bond needed to hold them together—perhaps the only bond. I am not speaking of God's chosen people, for whom the most extraordinary miracles and the most evident signs of grace took the place of human policy. But as it is the property of error to divide itself over and over *ad infinitum,* so knowledge based upon error turned men into a blind and fanatical crowd, pushing and jostling one another in a closed labyrinth, so that some sensitive and philosophical spirits have looked back with envy on man's former savage state. Such is the first epoch of history, in which learning, or, more properly speaking, opinion, is harmful.

The second epoch was the difficult and terrible transition from error to truth, from the darkness of the unknown to light. The mighty clash between the errors useful to a few powerful men and the truths that serve a host of weak ones, the concentration and ferment of passions which such an occasion calls forth, bring infinite harm to suffering humanity. Whoever reflects upon the histories of nations (the main epochs of which resemble one another after a certain period of time) will often find an entire generation sacrificed to the happiness of its successors in the sad but necessary passage from the shadows of ignorance to the light of truth and, consequently, from tyranny to liberty. But when spirits have been calmed and the fire that purged the nation of its oppressive evils has been extinguished, when truth, whose progress is slow at first and then more and more rapid, sits beside the throne of monarchs and is venerated by and has an altar in the parliaments of republics, then who will ever dare to assert that the light which enlightens the multitude is more harmful than darkness and that a solid understanding of the true and simple relationships of things is pernicious to men?

If blind ignorance is less deadly than mediocre and confused knowledge, which adds the errors that are unavoidable when one has a narrow view of the limits of truth to the evils of complete ignorance, then the most precious gift that a sovereign can give himself and the nation is to make an enlightened man the guardian and depository of the sacred laws. Accustomed to seeing the truth without fearing it, generally free of the need for reputation (which is scarcely ever satisfied and which puts the virtue of most men to the test), used to contemplating humanity from the loftiest point of view, from his perspective his own nation becomes a family linked by fraternal bonds, and the distance between the high and mighty and the common people seems all the less to him as the portion of mankind before his eyes is larger. Philosophers acquire needs and interests unknown to uneducated men; above all, philosophers do not recant in the public forum the principles that they have upheld in private, and they acquire the habit of loving truth for itself.[2] A good selection of such men constitutes the happiness of a nation, but that happiness will be temporary unless good laws augment their number so as to diminish the ever considerable risk of a poor choice.[3]

XLIII

MAGISTRATES[1]

Another way to prevent crimes is to make the corps of those charged with executing the law interested in observing rather than in corrupting it. The greater the number of men who constitute such a body, the less the danger of encroachments on the law will be, for venality is more difficult among magistrates who keep watch on one another, and their interest in increasing their personal authority is less to the degree that the share of power that would come to each of them is smaller, especially when compared to the danger of such an undertaking. If by his ostentation and pomp, by his edicts' severity, and by his refusing to grant a hearing to the just and unjust petitions of anyone who believes himself oppressed, the sovereign accustoms his subjects to fear the magistrates more than the laws, then the magistrates will profit from this fear more than personal or public security will gain from it.

XLIV

REWARDS

Another way of preventing crimes is to reward virtue. Upon this matter I observe a universal silence among the laws of all contemporary nations. If the prizes that academies award to those who discover useful truths have increased our knowledge and the number of good books, why should prizes distributed by the beneficent hand of the sovereign not increase virtuous deeds? The coin of honor is always inexhaustible and fruitful in the hands of one who distributes it wisely.

XLV

EDUCATION

Finally, the most certain but most difficult way to prevent crimes is to perfect education. This subject is too vast, and it exceeds the limits that I have set for myself. This topic, I even venture to say, is too intimately connected with the nature of government for it to remain a barren field cultivated only by a few sages until the remote future of social happiness. A great man who enlightens the world that persecutes him has shown in detail what the chief principles of an education truly useful to mankind are: it should consist, not of a sterile mass of subjects, but of a careful and precise selection of subjects; it should substitute originals for copies, both in the moral and physical phenomena that chance or diligence presents to the fresh minds of the young; it should lead youth to virtue by the easy path of feeling, and turn it away from evil by the infallible path of necessity and trouble, instead of using the uncertain method of command, which achieves only a feigned and temporary obedience.[1]

XLVI

PARDONS

To the degree that punishments become milder, clemency and pardon become less necessary. Happy the nation in which they would be pernicious! Clemency in a sovereign, then, that virtue which has sometimes been deemed a substitute for all the duties of the throne, ought to be excluded from a perfect law code, in which punishments would be mild and the means of adjudication regular and speedy. This truth will seem harsh to anyone who lives among the disorders of a system of criminal justice in which pardon and clemency are as necessary as the laws are absurd and as sentences are barbaric. This is the most beautiful prerogative of the throne, the most desirable attribute of sovereignty, and the tacit disapproval which beneficent administrators of public happiness show for a law code that, with all its imperfections, has in its favor the prejudice of centuries, the voluminous and imposing paraphernalia of an infinite number of commentators, the grave apparatus of endless formalities, and the support of the most insinuating and least formidable of the semi-educated. One should consider, however, that clemency is the virtue of the lawgiver and not of the executor of the law, that it ought to shine forth throughout the law code, not in particular judgments; that showing men that crimes may be pardoned and that punishment is not their inevitable consequence is to arouse the enticing hope of impunity; and that making people believe that, since remission is possible, sentences which go unremitted are violent acts of force rather than emanations of justice. What will be said, then, when the prince grants a pardon—that is, public security—to a private person and, with a private act of unenlightened benevolence, lays down a public decree of impunity?[1] Let the laws, therefore, be inexorable, and let those who enforce them be inexorable in individual cases, but let the lawgiver be gentle, indulgent, and humane. Let the legislator be a wise architect who raises his building on the foundation of self-love, and let the general interest be the result of the interests of every person; then he will not be constantly obliged to separate the public good from the good of private individuals with partial laws and remedies that cause riots; then he will not be compelled to build the image of public well-being on fear and mistrust. Let the profound philosopher, the philosopher of feeling, leave his fellow men to enjoy in peace that small portion of happiness which the immense system established by the First Cause, by Him Who *is*, allows them to enjoy in this corner of the universe.

XLVII

CONCLUSION

I conclude with the reflection that the magnitude of punishment ought to be relative to the condition of the nation itself. Stronger and more obvious impressions are required for the hardened spirits of a people who have scarcely emerged from a savage state. A thunderbolt is needed to fell a ferocious lion who is merely angered by a gun shot. But, to the extent that human spirits are made gentle by the social state, sensibility increases; as it increases, the severity of punishment must diminish if one wishes to maintain a constant relationship between object and feeling.[1]

From all that has been seen hitherto, one can deduce a very useful theorem, but one that scarcely conforms to custom, the usual lawgiver of nations. It is this: *In order that any punishment should not be an act of violence committed by one person or many against a private citizen; it is essential that it should be public, prompt, necessary, the minimum possible under the given circumstances, proportionate to the crimes, and established by law.//*

Translator's Notes

To The Reader

1. Beccaria's addition of "To the Reader" was prompted by the criticisms the essay had received, chiefly from Ferdinando Facchinei, a monk from Valombroso in Venetian territory. Facchinei condemned Beccaria's work on six charges of sedition and twenty-three of impiety. See Ferdinando Facchinei, *Note ed osservazioni sul libro intitolato "Dei delitti e delle pene"* (Venice, 1765). Excerpts from this book are printed in Cesare Beccaria, *Dei delitti e delle pene. Con una raccolta di lettere e documenti relativi alla nascita dell'opera e alla sua fortuna nell'Europa del Settecento*, ed. Franco Venturi (Turin, 1965), pp. 164–177. This edition of Beccaria's work with its valuable collection of documents hereafter will be cited as *Delitti* (Venturi ed.).

2. The Byzantine Emperor Justinian I, who reigned from 527 to 565, ordered a compilation of Roman law. Justinian's Code was received in western Europe in the Middle Ages, and, by Beccaria's day, it was the basis of most Continental legal systems.

3. The Lombards were a Germanic tribe who conquered a good deal of Italy and who gave their name to Beccaria's native province. Their laws served as the basis of much later jurisprudence, especially in Milan and the surrounding area.

4. Benedict Carpzov (1595–1666), Giulio Claro (1525–1575) and Prospero Farinacci (1544–1618) were legal commentators whose opinions carried great authority. As Beccaria's grandson, Alessandro Manzoni, pointed out, these and other commentators actually tried to reduce the savagery of judicial proceedings, but they never repudiated Roman law or suggested that torture as such was illegitimate. Alessandro Manzoni, *Storia della colonna infame*, in Allessandro Manzoni, *Opere*, ed. Ricardo Bacchelli (Milan, 1953), pp. 973–986.

5. Beccaria here refers to the Austrian regime in Lombardy. Under Maria Theresa (1740–1780), Joseph II (1780–1790), and Leopold II (1790–1792), the Austrian government launched a series of reform programs with which Beccaria and his friends were eager to cooperate. Ottavio Barriè, *La cultura politica nell'età delle riforme*, in *Storia di Milano* (Fondazione Treccani degli Alfieri per la Storia di Milano; Giovanni Treccani degli Alfieri, dir.), vol. 12, *L'età delle riforme, 1706–1796* (Milan, 1959), pp. 596–640.

6. Beccaria is referring primarily to Facchinei.

7. The claim that all moral systems could be reduced to utilitarianism had been advanced by Helvétius, whose work greatly influenced Beccaria, and was later elaborated by Bentham. Claude Helvétius, *De l'esprit* (Paris, 1759), disc. 2, chaps. 1, 6, 13, pp. 33–37, 57–62, 97–104; Jeremy Bentham, *An Introduction to the Principles of Morals and Legislation*, ed. J. H. Burns and H. L. A. Hart (London, 1970), chap. 1, secs. 1–2, p. 11; chap. 2, pp. 17–33.

8. It was a common eighteenth-century belief that Thomas Hobbes had held that primitive men are inherently wicked and self-seeking, and Beccaria followed the view that Hobbes spoke of original men in the state of nature. More recent commentators, however, have held that, when Hobbes wrote about the state of nature, he had in mind what his contemporaries would be like if there were no government. Thomas Hobbes, *Leviathan*, ed. C. B. Macpherson (London, 1968), bk 1, chaps. 13–14, pp. 183–201; C. B. Macpherson, *The Politics of Possessive Individualism, Hobbes to Locke* (Oxford, 1964), pp. 21–29.

9. Early in 1765, Pietro and Alessandro Verri published a point-by-point reply to Facchinei. Beccaria refers to it here as though it were his. See Pietro Verri and Alessandro Verri, *Risposta ad uno scritto che s'intitola Note ed osservazioni sul libro "Dei delitti e delle pene"* (Lugano, 1765), excerpted in *Delitti* (Ventri ed.), pp. 178–186.

10. The additions in question were made in the second and third editions, both published at Leghorn, though with false place impressions. Sergi Romagnoli, "Nota," to Cesare Beccaria, *Dei delitti e delle pene*, in Cesare Beccaria, *Opere*, ed. Sergio Ramagnoli (Florence, 1958), 1:38–39.

Introduction

1. Many origins for this utilitarian phrasing have been suggested. One commonly mentioned is Francis Hutcheson, who, in his *Inquiry Concerning Moral Good and Evil* (London, 1726) had maintained, "That action is best, which procures the greatest happiness for the greatest numbers; and that worst, which in like manner, occasions misery" (pp. 177–178). A more immediate source, however, was probably Beccaria's friend, Pietro Verri, who had spoken of "the greatest possible happiness divided with the greatest possible equality" in his *Meditazioni sulla felicità*, originally published in 1763. See Pietro Verri, *Discorso sulla felicità*, ed. Enrico Emanuelli (Milan, 1944), p. 58. See also Franco Venturi, *Settecento riformatore. Da Muratori a Beccaria* (Turin, 1969), p. 706.

2. In the eithteenth century, it was common among Enlightenment writers to praise capitalistic competition as an alternative to vainglorious warfare. In particular, Pietro Verri spoke of economic competition as "the real war" that civilized

men, especially Lombards, should fight. See Pietro Verri, "Elementi del commercio," in Pietro Verri et al., *Il caffè, ossia brevi e vari discorsi distribuiti in fogli periodici,* ed. Sergio Romagnoli (Milan, 1960), pp. 27–32. See also Albert O. Hirschman, *The Passions and the Interests: Political Arguments for Capitalism before Its Triumph* (Princeton, 1977), pp. 9–14, 56–66.

3. Montesquieu did suggest a number of improvements in criminal procedure, notably milder and more humane punishments and an end to judicial torture. Montesquieu, however, praised the rights of the nobility and the power of intermediary bodies, whereas Beccaria was a spokesman for enlightened absolutism. See Montesquieu, *De l'esprit des lois,* in Montesquieu, *Oeuvres complètes* ed. Roger Caillois vol. 2 (Paris, 1951), bk. 2, chap. 4, pp. 247–249; bk. 5, chap. 11, pp. 290–291; bk. 6, pp. 307–332; bk. 8, chaps. 5–8, pp. 353–356; bk. 12, pp. 433–458. Beccaria declared that he owed his own "conversion to philosophy" to reading Montesquieu's *Persian Letters.* Beccaria to Morellet, 26 Jan. 1766, in *Opere* (Romagnoli ed.), 2:865. On the relationship of Beccaria's work to Enlightenment social thought generally, see Philip Jenkins, "Varieties of Enlightenment Criminology," *The British Journal of Criminology* 24 (1984):112–130.

Chapter I

1. The idea of laws as conditions of the social contract was fundamental to Rousseau. Jean-Jacques Rousseau, *Du contrat social,* in Jean-Jacques Rousseau, *Oeuvres complètes,* ed. Bernard Gagnebin and Marcel Raymond, vol. 3 (Paris, 1964), bk. 2, chap. 6, pp. 378–380.

2. This view of human nature as motivated chiefly by self-interest was common among eighteenth-century utilitarians. Helvétius had declared that all men seek to become despots and that tangible motives are necessary to check this tendency. Helvétius, *De l'esprit,* disc. 3, chap. 17, pp. 284–289. Beccaria frankly admitted that he owed a large part of his ideas to Helvétius. Beccaria to Morellet, 26 Jan. 1766, in *Opere* (Romagnoli ed.), 2:865. Kant and Hegel, of course, vehemently objected to such a theory of punishment, and it must be noted that it was not always typical of Beccaria. Immanuel Kant, *The Metaphysical Elements of Justice. Part I of the Metaphysics of Morals,* ed. and trans. John Ladd (Indianapolis, 1965), p. 100; G. W. F. Hegel, *Hegel's Philosophy of Right,* ed. and trans. T. M. Knox (London, 1967), p. 246.

Chapter II

1. Montesquieu had held that excessive and unnecessary penalties are suitable only for a despotic government. Montesquieu, *De l'esprit des lois* (Caillois ed.), bk. 6, chap. 9, 2:318–319.

2. This account of the formation of societies closely parallels the one which Montesquieu gave in his *De l'esprit des lois* (Caillois ed.), bk. 1, chap. 3, 2:236–238.

3. Beccaria's account of the social contract is quite unlike the total surrender of rights of which Rousseau spoke. Rousseau, *Du contrat social* (Gagnebin and Raymond ed.), bk. 1, chap. 6, 3:360–362. It is, rather, much closer to Locke's idea that the sovereign is purely fiduciary and that the people forming a state make only a minimal surrender of their liberty. John Locke, *The Second Treatise of Government*, ed. Thomas P. Peardon (Indianapolis, 1952), chap. 3, para. 21, p. 14; chap. 8, paras. 95–101, pp. 54–57.

4. Beccaria's utilitarian view of justice appears very similar to the ideas expounded by Helvétius. Helvétius, *De l'esprit*, (1759 ed.), disc. 2, chap. 5, pp. 55–57; chap. 8, pp. 69–74; chap. 12, pp. 89–97.

Chapter III

1. Rousseau, who had an immense influence on Beccaria, insisted that only the sovereign, representing the general will, has the right to establish laws. Rousseau, *Du contrat social* (Gagnebin and Raymond ed.), bk. 1, chap. 7, 3:362–363; bk. 2, chap. 1, 3:368–369.

2. Rousseau maintained that the general will, the sovereign legislator, could lay down only general laws and could not apply them in particular cases; doing that, Rousseau declared, was the task of the magistrate. Rousseau, *Du contrat social*, bk. 2, chap. 4, 3:372–375.

Chapter IV

1. The entire chapter is a reaction against the unbridled judicial discretion characteristic of Beccaria's day. With the blend of Roman law, local custom, royal decrees, judicial commentaries, and court precedent which constituted the legal systems in most of Europe, judges had all but total authority to decide what laws would be applied and to whom. A good account of this is to be found in Manzoni, *Opere* (Bacchelli ed.), pp. 973–989. Voltaire discovered this state of affairs in his campaign for law reform in France. Peter Gay, *Voltaire's Politics: The Poet as Realist* (New York, 1965), pp. 294–296. Conservatives, however, argued that a wide scope for interpretation reinforced a benevolent paternalistic power of the upper classes. See Facchinei, *Note ed osservazioni*, pp. 13–14, 16, 23–24.

2. Montesquieu had inveighed against the degeneration of an aristocracy into an oligarchy, deeming the latter a despotism with many despots. Montesquieu, *De l'esprit des lois* (Caillois ed.), bk. 8, chap. 5, 2:353–354. Though Beccaria may have

wished to elaborate on Montesquieu's theme, his target was obviously the aristocracy, particularly the older generation of the Milanese patriciate. See Daniel M. Klang, "Reform and Enlightenment in Eighteenth-Century Lombardy," *Canadian Journal of History/Annales Canadiennes d'Histoire* 19 (1984): 39–70.

Chapter V

1. In Beccaria's day, laws were promulgated in Latin in much of Europe. Maria Theresa's criminal code of 1770 was drawn up in Latin and picturesquely named the *Nemesis Teresiana*. Some decades after Beccaria, Hegel deplored the practice of couching laws in a dead tongue. Hegel, *Philosophy of Right* (Knox ed.), p. 138.

2. This statement may be interpreted as a jab at Montesquieu, who held that a monarchy required a special intermediary body, such as the French *parlements* or the Senate of Milan, to serve as a depository of law. Montesquieu, *De l'esprit des lois* (Caillois ed.), bk. 2, chap. 5, 2:249.

3. In the eighteenth century, many writers defended the growth of wealth and luxury as sources of virtue. Hirschman, *Passions and Interests,* pp. 14–18. Among those with whom Beccaria was best acquainted, Helvétius, and, following him, Pietro Verri, had mounted especially strong arguments in favor of luxury. Helvétius, *De l'esprit* (1759 ed.), disc. 1, chap. 3, pp. 12–24; Pietro Verri, *Meditazioni sulla economia politica,* in Pietro Verri, *Opere filosofiche e di economia politica* (Milan, 1835), 1:155–364; Pietro Verri, "Considerazioni sul lusso," in *Il caffè* (Romagnoli ed.), pp. 113–118.

4. Among Italian conservatives in general and older Lombard patricians in particular, it was common to deem the eighteenth century "corrupt" because of the growth of prosperity and the infusion of transalpine ideas. Venturi, *Settecento riformatore,* p. 657. Pietro Verri lampooned this outlook in his "Orazione panegirica sulla giurisprudenza milanese," written in 1763. This is printed in *Delitti* (Venturi ed.), pp. 127–146; see esp. pp. 127–129.

Chapter VI

1. Bentham later elaborated on this theme at great length. Bentham, *Principles* (Burns and Hart ed.), chap. 14, secs. 1–14, pp. 165–169.

2. The decline of public–spirited virtue as a necessary consequence of excessive expansion was a central theme in Montesquieu's analysis of Roman history. Montesquieu, *Considérations sur les causes de la grandeur des romains et de leur décadence,* in *Oeuvres* (Caillois ed.), vol. 2, chaps. 9–12, 2:116–136.

3. This analysis of the role of the legislator is very close to the one Helvétius expounded. Helvétius, *De l'esprit* (1759 ed.), disc. 2, chaps. 15-17, pp. 115-130.

4. This view of human motivation was, of course, typical of utilitarians both before and after Beccaria. Helvétius, *De l'esprit*, disc. 3, chaps. 8-9, pp. 227-243; Bentham, *Principles* (Burns and Hart ed.), chaps. 1-2, pp. 11-37.

5. Montesquieu had declared, "It is essential that punishments be proportional to one another because it is essential to avoid a great crime rather than a lesser one, a crime which attacks society more rather than one which disturbs it less . . . In Muscovy, where the punishment for robbers is the same as for assassins, murders are a daily occurrence. The dead, they say there, tell no tales." Montesquieu, *De l'esprit des lois* (Caillois ed.), bk. 6, chap. 16, 2:327-328; see also bk. 12, chap. 4, 2:433-435.

Chapter VII

1. This paragraph is directly contrary to the view later advocated by Kant, that the state of the criminal's will is the ultimate standard of the seriousness of his offense. Kant, *Justice* (Ladd ed.), pp. 99-102.

2. Church and state were closely linked in Beccaria's day, and there was often little distinction between sin and crime. Conservatives generally maintained that religion was essential for social order. Facchinei, *Note ed osservazioni*, pp. 13-28.

3. Montesquieu had proclaimed, "We must honor the Divinity, however, and never avenge Him. In effect, if we were to be guided by this latter idea, what would be the end of punishments? If the laws of men had to avenge an infinite Being, they would be regulated by His infinity and not by the weakness, ignorance, and caprice of human nature." Montesquieu, *De l'esprit des lois* (Caillois ed.), bk. 12, chap. 4, 2:434.

Chapter VIII

1. The division of crimes that Beccaria offers is similar to, and perhaps inspired by, Montesquieu's chapter on the same subject. Montesquieu, *De l'esprit des lois* (Caillois ed.), bk. 12, chap. 4, 433-435.

2. Though Hegel rejected any utilitarian foundation of the right to punish, it is noteworthy that he was at one with Beccaria in declaring that the social harm of an offense is the only way of measuring its relative importance. Like Beccaria, Hegel held that the relative importance of specific crimes might vary precisely because their impact could differ in different times and places. Hegel, *Philosophy of Right* (Knox ed.), pp. 68-72, 274.

3. This passage may well have been inspired by Montesquieu's definition of liberty as "the right to do everything that the law permits." Montesquieu, *De l'esprit des lois* (Caillois ed.) bk. 11, chap. 3, 2:395.

4. This view of man's complete animal-like natural freedom was expounded by Rousseau in his *Discours sur l'origine et les fondements de l'inégalité parmi les hommes.* See *Oeuvres* (Gagnebin and Raymond ed.), 3:141-155; see also *Du contrat social,* bk. 1, chaps. 1-6, 3:351-362.

Chapter IX

1. Kant later presented a discussion of honor remarkably similar to Beccaria's, declaring that disputes over points of honor placed the parties involved outside the bounds of legal justice and in a state of nature. Kant, *Justice* (Ladd ed.), pp. 106-107.

2. Montesquieu had held that honor—a sense of one's own worth and of the dignity of one's rank—is fundamental in monarchies. Montesquieu, however, could not conceive of honor having any place in an arbitrary despotism or in a republic. Beccaria accepted Montesquieu's analysis, but he had a far lower opinion of monarchy, nobility, and honor than did the Frenchman. Montesquieu, *De l'esprit des lois* (Caillois ed.), bk. 3, chaps. 3-8, 2:251-258.

Chapter X

1. Kant was at one with Beccaria in holding that a man, especially a junior military officer, who fought a duel and killed the party who had slighted his honor, could not be said to have committed murder. As long as existing laws and insitutions permitted and encouraged disputes over points of honor, so long as the law provided no recourse for the offended party, duelling would have to be beyond the purview of criminal justice. Kant, *Justice* (Ladd ed.), pp. 106-107.

Chapter XI

1. Like the other members of the Verri circle, Beccaria saw it as his mission to introduce Enlightenment ideas from abroad into what he deemed a backward Italy. Beccaria to Morellet, 26 Jan. 1766, in *Opere* (Romagnoli ed.), 2:862, 866.

2. John Adams quoted this passage to excellent effect in his defense of the British soldiers in the Boston Massacre trial of 1770. Marcello Maestro, *Cesare Beccaria and the Origins of Penal Reform* (Philadelphia, 1973), pp. 137-138.

Chapter XII

1. Beccaria showed his most utilitarian side in discussing the purpose of punishment. In this regard, Bentham followed in his footsteps, while Kant and Hegel deplored these principles. Bentham, *Principles* (Burns and Hart ed.), chap. 13, pp. 158–164; Kant, *Justice,* p. 100; Hegel, *Philosophy of Right,* p. 246. On Beccaria's belief that punishment should achieve the maximum mental impact with the least cost in physical pain, see Michel Foucault, *Discipline and Punish: The Birth of the Prison,* trans. Alan Sheridan (New York, 1977), pp. 73–103.

Chapter XIII

1. Just how flimsy such conjectures could be was shown by the condemnation of several Milanese in 1630 for allegedly spreading the plague by smearing walls with a pestiferous ointment. There was no plausible motive for such gratuitous malice, and the evidence presented would have been laughable had it not led to terrible suffering. Manzoni, *Colonna infame, passim.*

2. Beccaria's grandson discussed at some length the great authority that commentators exercised in the absence of a clear system of jurisprudence. Manzoni, *Colonna infame,* pp. 973–975, 986.

3. Montesquieu had devoted an important chapter to undercutting the bases of accusations of sorcery. He was circumspect, however, for sorcery was still a legal offense in many countries in the mid–eighteenth century. Montesquieu, *De l'esprit des lois* (Caillois ed.), bk. 12, chap. 5, 2:435–436; see also Gay, *Voltaire's Politics,* p. 290.

4. Helvétius had devoted several chapters to the baneful effects of private societies, and Beccaria appears to echo him here. Helvétius, *De l'esprit* (Knox ed.), disc. 2, chaps. 7–9, pp. 62–81.

5. Montesquieu bitterly opposed making indiscrete words into criminal acts, especially in cases of lese majesty. Montesquieu, *De l'esprit des lois* (Caillois ed.), bk. 12, chap. 12, 2:443–444. It is such cases that Beccaria probably had in mind in this instance.

Chapter XIV

1. Beccaria's praise of trial by jury may well be based on Montesquieu's esteem for this English practice. Montesquieu, however, was inaccurate in stating that an English judge had no other function than to pronounce the legally established sentence once the jury had decided the facts of the case. Montesquieu, *De l'esprit des lois* (Caillois ed.), bk. 6, chap. 3, 2:311.

Chapter XV

1. Despite Beccaria's disclaimer, this chapter is directed especially against Venice, where the state inquisitors received secret accusations against seditious or ambitious citizens in order to foil plots against the oligarchy that controlled the Republic. This chapter was among those that prompted Facchinei, with the blessings of the Venetian authorities, to write his diatribe against Beccaria. Facchinei, *Note ed Osservazioni*, pp. 49–58. Montesquieu had written at some length on this Venetian custom, but he had praised secret accusations there, arguing that they were a necessary means of preserving the republic's liberty. Montesquieu, *De l'esprit des lois* (Caillois ed.), bk. 2, chap. 3, 2:245–246; bk. 5, chap. 8, 2:286–287; bk. 11, chap. 6, 2:397. Beccaria, a Milanese and therefore closer to Venice, had a much lower opinion of the reputed wisdom of the Republic than did Montesquieu.

2. Montesquieu wrote of the methods of accusation under various types of government in *De l'esprit des lois* (Caillois ed.), bk. 6, chap. 8, 2:317.

Chapter XVI

1. Before Beccaria, Montesquieu had deplored the use of judicial torture, which was common in most places on the Continent. Montesquieu had held that this practice is suitable only in despotic states and that careful investigation, not a forced confession, is the only way to obtain evidence against a criminal. Montesquieu, *De l'esprit des lois* (Caillois ed.), bk. 6, chap. 17, 2:329; bk. 29, chap. 11, 2:872. Pietro Verri had already begun to work on his largely utilitarian denunciation of torture while Beccaria was writing his book, though Verri's work was not completed until 1777 and not published until 1804. See Pietro Verri, *Osservazioni sulla tortura*, ed. Plinio Succhetto (Bologna, 1962), pp. 177–280.

2. Pietro Verri employed precisely the same argument in his "Orazione panegirica sulla giurisprudenza milanese," *Delitti* (Venturi ed.), pp. 132–133. On the efforts of Enlightenment reformers generally to introduce new criteria of judicial certainty, see Foucault, *Discipline and Punish*, pp. 38–43, 79–82.

3. As Beccaria's grandson explained, torture was originally applied to persons who were deemed disreputable and who accused other persons of crimes. Pain, it was held, gave such testimony a credibility that the accuser's character did not. Torture, of course, was applied to suspects as well as accusers. Manzoni, *Colonna infame*, pp. 1009–1010.

4. Torture became more common from the eleventh century onward. Ecclesiastical courts held that a confession, even if extracted under torture, was essential for the salvation of the criminal's soul, but the practice was quickly taken up by secular magistrates. Pietro Verri's discussion of the matter was very similar to Beccaria's in his *Osservazioni sulla tortura*, pp. 259–263.

5. The psychology employed here by Beccaria was common in the eighteenth century, and it leads him to a very dubious account of the relationship between judicial torture and trials by ordeal. In particular, Helvétius had argued the points on which Beccaria relies. Helvétius, *De l'esprit* (1759 ed.), disc. 3, chaps. 1-2, pp. 187-194.

6. As Melchoir Grimm, a sympathetic critic, noted, Beccaria's language was "sometimes too geometrical." See Grimm's review of the French translation of Beccaria's book in his *Correspondance littéraire*, 1 Dec. 1765, excerpted in *Delitti* (Venturi ed.), p. 340. Beccaria's propensity to calculate pleasure and pain mathematically probably endeared him to Bentham more than anything else. Bentham, of course, carried the propensity to extremes. See esp. Bentham, *Principles* (Burns and Hart ed.), chaps. 4-6, pp. 38-73.

7. Manzoni later gave an excellent brief discussion of the Roman practice of using torture only against slaves. Manzoni, *Colonna infame*, p. 1022.

8. Montesquieu had commented on and praised the absence of torture in English jurisprudence. Montesquieu, *De l'esprit des lois* (Caillois ed.), bk. 19, chap. 11, 2:872.

9. Torture in common criminal cases was abolished in Sweden in 1734, but Gustavus III, claiming Beccaria as his mentor, abolished it altogether in 1772. Domenico Michelesi to Bonomo Algarotti, 2 Sept. 1772, in *Delitti* (Venturi ed.), p. 629.

10. Frederick II of Prussia abolished judicial torture when he ascended the throne in 1740.

11. It was indeed a common opinion among jurists that a suspect who confessed under torture had to reconfirm his confession on another day and out of sight of the instruments of torture. Legal commentators had tried to limit the use of torture in this manner, but they generally held that a prisoner who did not confirm his earlier testimony could be tortured again. Manzoni, *Colonna infame*, p. 1021.

12. Though Voltaire generally agreed with Beccaria's condemnation of torture, he did favor retaining it as a means of discovering the accomplices of particularly dangerous or brutal criminals. Voltaire, *Prix de la justice et de l'humanité* (Geneva, 1778), excerpted in *Delitti* (Venturi ed.), pp. 493-495. Voltaire apparently missed Beccaria's two central points: that torture, in any case whatsoever, is ineffective and also contrary to the natural right of self-defense.

Chapter XVII

1. In the early Middle Ages, most punishments were indeed fines; these constituted a considerable portion of royal revenues. In the eighteenth century, David

Hume, for one, explored this topic at length. Hume's comments on the subject are found in his discussion of Anglo-Saxon law. David Hume, *History of England* (Philadelphia, 1821), vol. 1, chap. 1, pp. 136-140.

Chapter XVIII

1.   In Beccaria's day, forcing an accused person to testify against himself under oath was as common as judicial torture. Montesqieu was one of several writers who had condemned this practice as contrary to the natural right of self-defense. Montesquieu, *De l'esprit des lois* (Caillois ed.), bk. 6, chap. 13, 2:322. Beccaria condemns forced self-incrimination, whether by oath or by torture, as contrary to the right of self-defense as well as on grounds of expedience. On the social functions of compelling a criminal to confess, see Foucault, *Discipline and Punish,* pp. 32-45.

Chapter XX

1.   Montesquieu had stressed the difference in crimes against persons and against property, and he had argued that different sorts of punishment ought to be applied to each. Montesquieu, *De l'esprit des lois* (Caillois ed.), bk. 12, chap. 4, 2:635. By "corporal penalties" (*pene corporali*) in this context, Beccaria does not necessarily mean what is usually called "corporal punishment," but rather any chastisement that affects the person rather than the property of the offender. In this sense, imprisonment would be a "corporal penalty."

2.   Kant, who declared that persons should always be treated as ends in themselves and never as means to anything, was no doubt pleased with this passage. Like Beccaria—and for similar reasons—Kant insisted that the rich should never be able to atone for offenses against the poor simply by paying fines. Kant, *Justice* (Ladd ed.), pp. 101-102.

Chapter XXI

1.   This passage is an obvious attack on Montesquieu's contention that a privileged hereditary nobility is essential to a monarchy, a necessary buffer between the sovereign and the common people. Montesquieu, *De l'esprit des lois* (Caillois ed.), bk. 2, chap. 4, 2:247-249. The members of the Academy of Fists were especially hostile to the aristocratic practice of entailing estates, making their lands perpetually indivisible and inalienable. This, the reformers argued, stifled economic development and the circulation of wealth. See esp. Alfonso Longo, "Osservazioni su i fede commessi," in *Il caffè* (Romagnoli ed.), pp. 86-97; see also Klang, "Reform and Enlightenment," pp. 39-43, 60-63.

2. The egalitarian individualism expressed here is clearly influenced by Rousseau. See Rousseau, *Du contrat social* (Gagnebin and Raymond ed.), bk. 2, chap. 6, 3:378–380. Many of Beccaria's critics recognized the Genevan's influence, and Facchinei, intending no compliment, dubbed Beccaria, "the Rousseau of the Italians." Facchinei, *Note ed osservazioni*, p. 188.

3. In a memorandum prepared for the Austrian government in 1791, Beccaria appeared to renege on this commitment to equality of penalties, arguing that persons of quality should be exempted from "degrading punishments" (*pene infamante*) because of their special sensibilities. Cesare Beccaria, "Brevi riflessione intorno al codice generale sopra i delitti e le pene, per cio che riguarda i delitti politici," (1791) in *Opere* (Romagnoli ed.), 2:709–710. On the relationship of criminal law reform (and its limitations) to the economic and political reforms that Beccaria and his friends wanted, see Drew Humphries and David F. Greenberg, "The Dialetics of Crime Control," in *Crime and Capitalism*, ed. David F. Greenberg (Palto Alto, Cal., 1981), pp. 223–224.

Chapter XXII

1. Beccaria always insisted that the right of private property is social, not natural, and that the sovereign can limit it if the public good requires. In his lectures on political economy, for instance, he vehemently denied that the rights of property are absolute, and, in particular, he held that the sovereign may closely supervise private woodlands for the sake of conservation. He also argued that the sovereign could act against what he regarded as socially harmful forms of property, notably mortmain and entails. Cesare Beccaria, *Elementi di economia pubblica*, in *Opere* (Romagnoli ed.), 1:442–443, 493–495, 507–508.

2. Beccaria later came to reject punishments such as flogging and the pillory on several grounds, chiefly because he deemed them inherently degrading. Beccaria, "Brevi riflessione intorno al codice generale," in *Opere* (Romagnoli ed.), 2:705–718.

3. Montesquieu, for one, had underscored this point. Montesquieu, *De l'esprit des lois* (Caillois ed.), bk. 6, chap. 16, 2:328.

Chapter XXIII

1. Beccaria returned to this point in his memorandum of 1791 on degrading punishments, arguing that shame and disgrace should always arise from the crime itself, never from the punishment. Beccaria, "Brevi riflessione intorno al codice generale," in *Opere* (Romagnoli ed.), 2:710–711.

2. Beccaria later wrote and published the first portion of a projected larger work on style. His ideas on aesthetics, however, were not well developed, and the essay did not enjoy an enthusiastic response. Beccaria, *Ricerche intorno alla natura dello stile,* in *Opere* (Romagnoli ed.), 1:197–336.

Chapter XXIV

1. This chapter is clearly directed against contemplative monastic orders. During the reign of Joseph II, the Austrian government abolished all contemplative orders in Lombardy. Needless to say, this chapter aroused the special ire of Facchinei. Facchinei, *Note ed osservazioni,* 79–88.

2. Once again, Beccaria showed his adherence to the Enlightenment view, one advocated especially by Pietro Verri, that luxury is desirable and that economic competition is an excellent substitute for warfare. Venturi, *Settecento riformatore,* pp. 668–669, 729. Beccaria's critics disliked his emphasis on economic virtues and instead praised the religious and military virtues characteristic of a traditional elite. Facchinei, *Note ed osservazioni,* pp. 30–32.

Chapter XXV

1. Confiscation of a convicted criminal's property was common in the eighteenth century. Before Beccaria, Montesquieu had deplored wholesale confiscations on the grounds that they were arbitrary, injurious to the innocent, and suitable only in despotic countries. Montesquieu, *De l'esprit des lois* (Caillois ed.), bk. 5, chap. 16, 2:298–299.

2. Statements such as this make it clear that Beccaria was by no means a thoroughgoing utilitarian. This passage is in the same spirit as Kant's later assertion, "Judicial punishment can never be used merely as a means to promote some other good for the criminal himself or for civil society ... He must first be found deserving of punishment before any thought can be given to the utility of this punishment for himself or for his fellow citizens." Kant, *Justice* (Ladd ed.), p. 100.

Chapter XXVI

1. The entire chapter reflects the "generation gap" of the Lombard Enlightenment. Cesare's father, Giovanni Beccaria, had deplored his son's marriage with Teresa Blasco, put the young man under house arrest for a time, and finally cut off his son and daughter-in-law, allowing them only a modest pension. Eventually there was a reconciliation, but Cesare rejected the world of his father, the world of a

traditional patrician, and he never accepted the custom–sanctioned authority of a
paterfamilias. Maestro, *Cesare Beccaria,* pp. 5–12. Similarly, Pietro Verri repudiated
the conservative, judicial, precedent-saturated outlook of his father, Senator Gabriele
Verri.

2.   Many social contract writers had indeed viewed society as a union of
households rather than of individuals as such. See, *inter alia,* Hobbes, *Leviathan* (Macpherson ed.), pt. 1, chap. 13, p. 187; Locke, *Second Treatise* (Peardon ed.), chap. 6,
paras. 73–75, pp. 41–43; chap. 8, para, 110, p. 63.

3.   Of all the social contract writers, Rousseau had most vehemently denied
that the family could serve as a political unit or the foundation for civil authority.
Rousseau, *Du contrat social,* bk. 1, chaps. 2–5, pp. 352–359. Locke had done so too,
though to a far lesser extent. Locke, *Second Treatise* (Peardon ed.), chap. 6, pp. 30–44.

4.   Once again, Beccaria appears to be influenced by Montesquieu's account of the decline of Rome. Montesquieu, *Considérations sur la grandeur des romains* (Caillois ed.), chaps. 8–12, 2:111–136.

5.   Lucius Cornelius Sulla, noted for his ambition, was Dictator of Rome
from 82 to 79 B.C. Beccaria probably intended this passage as a tribute to Pietro Verri.
Some members of the Academy of Fists adopted the names of classical figures whose
characters resembled their own. Beccaria took the name of Titus Pomponius Atticus, a
modest, quiet, and studious philosopher. Pietro Verri was known as Sulla because of
his ambition for public office, his support of absolutism, and his desire to introduce
sweeping changes. Beccaria's description of the philosophical, despotic dictator appears to be an idealized version of Pietro Verri. Venturi, *Settecento riformatore,*
pp. 683–684.

Chapter XXVII

1.   On several occasions, Montesquieu remarked that cruel punishments
are suitable only in a despotic state, which is based upon fear, and that excessive
penalties are most likely to be found in such a regime. Montesquieu, *Lettres persanes*
(Caillois ed.), vol. 1 (Paris, 1949) letter 80, pp. 252–253; Montesquieu, *De l'esprit des
lois,* bk. 12, chap. 4, 2:433–435.

2.   Breaking on the wheel was a common form of execution in the eighteenth century. An English traveler in France described such an execution: "On the
scaffold was erected a large cross exactly in the form of that commonly represented for
Saint Andrew's. The executioner and his assistants then placed the prisoner on it, in
such a manner that his arms and legs were extended exactly agreeable to the form of
the cross, and strongly tied down; under each arm, leg, etc., was cut a notch in the

wood, as a mark where the executioner might strike, and break the bone with greater facility. He held in his hand a large iron bar . . . and in the first place broke his arms, then in a moment after both his thighs; it was a melancholy, shocking sight, to see him heave his body up and down in extreme agony, and hideous to behold the terrible distortions of his face; it was a considerable time before he expired. . . ." Sacheverell Stevens, *Miscellaneous Remarks Made on . . . France, Italy, Germany, and Holland* (London, 1756) as cited in Jeffry Kaplow, *The Names of Kings: The Parisian Laboring Poor in the Eighteenth Century* (New York, 1972), p. 135.

3. Bentham later elaborated on this calculation of the excess of harm over the profit of the crime, citing Beccaria in the process. Bentham, *Principles* (Burns and Hart ed.), chap. 14, pp. 165–174, esp. sec. 8, n.

4. Montesquieu had made precisely this point as early as 1721. Montesquieu, *Lettres persanes* (Caillois ed.), letter 80, 1:252–253.

5. The point Beccaria is making here is based on the psychology of Helvétius, Helvétius, *De l'esprit* (1759 ed.), disc. 1, pp. 1–32; disc. 3, chaps. 1–3, pp. 187–202.

Chapter XXVIII

1. Beccaria's detractors were quick to seize on this argument. Facchinei, for instance, suggested that one could just as well argue that no one would ever grant the sovereign the right to punish him in any way. Facchinei, *Note ed osservazioni*, pp. 105–106. Thoroughgoing utilitarians, while perhaps sympathetic to Beccaria's conclusions, deplored his contractarian arguments. See, for instance, Melchior Grimm's review of the French translation in his *Correspondance littéraire* of 1 Dec. 1765, in *Delitti* (Venturi ed.), pp. 343–344.

2. In arguing that the death penalty is an act of war, Beccaria is, in effect, saying that it is an act of annihilation, not of coercion. One may very well argue that the state has the right to coerce, but capital punishment itself (as opposed to the *threat* of capital punishment) is not coercion at all. It is certainly possible to develop arguments against the death penalty on contractarian grounds. See, for instance, Thomas W. Satre, "The Irrationality of Capital Punishment," *The Southwestern Journal of Philosophy* 6 (1975): 75–87.

3. Rousseau, who may have influenced Beccaria's views on capital punishment, wrote, "There is no right to put someone to death, even in order to set an example, unless he cannot be kept alive without danger." Rousseau, *Du contrat social* (Gagnebin and Raymond ed.), bk. 2, chap. 5, 3:377.

4.   Czarina Elizabeth I, who reigned from 1741 to 1762, was opposed to the death penalty and abolished it with two separate decrees in 1753 and 1754.

5.   Passages such as this show Beccaria at his most utilitarian, thinking of the criminal merely as an object lesson rather than a person. Beccaria later rejected sentences of public labor for minor crimes, and he implied that public labor, since it is inherently degrading, should not be used as a punishment for any offense. Beccaria, "Brevi riflessione intorno al codice generale," in *Opere* (Romagnoli ed.), 2:709–711, 717.

6.   In the eighteenth century, it was common for the disadvantaged (from whose ranks most criminals came) to feel sympathy or curiosity at the sight of a public execution. Rarely, if ever, did such a spectacle inspire "salutary fear." Foucault, *Discipline and Punish*, pp. 54–68, 104–131: Kaplow, *Names of Kings*, pp. 136–137.

7.   Here Beccaria states an important principle of retributivist theories of punishment, especially those of a contractarian sort: if a criminal is punished because he violated an ostensibly universally beneficial system of rules, there is no reason that he should have felt bound by those rules in the first place if they caused him to bear many burdens and receive few benefits. See esp. Herbert Morris, "Persons and Punishment," in *Punishment and Rehabilitation,* ed. Jeffrie G. Murphy (Belmont, Cal., 1973), p. 56.

8.   Beccaria's description of valid laws is quite similar to Rousseau's account of the legislative general will. Rousseau, *Du contrat social* (Gagnebin and Raymond ed.), bk. 2, chap. 3, 3:371–372; chaps. 6–7, 3:378–384.

9.   These Roman emperors of the first and second centuries were famous for their concern for the happiness and well-being of their people.

10.   Once more, Beccaria takes aim at the aristocratic intermediary bodies, such as the French *parlements* or the Senate of Milan, which Montesquieu had praised so highly.

11.   In 1792, Beccaria prepared a memorandum on the death penalty for the Austrian government. He repeated most of the arguments in this chapter, and he added a new one: unlike other punishments, the death penalty is absolutely irrevocable. Therefore, he contended, it should be inflicted only in cases of total certainty. Since humans are not infallible, however, Beccaria concluded that there could never be sufficient certainty to warrant the use of capital punishment. Cesare Beccaria, "Vota . . . per la riforma del sistema criminale nella Lombardia austriaca riguardante la pena di morte" (1792) in *Opere* (Romagnoli ed.), 2:735–741. This is one of the strongest arguments against the death penalty; modern opponents of capital punishment have developed it and relied heavily upon it. See esp. Jeffrie G. Murphy, "Cruel and Unusual Punishments," in *Retribution, Justice, and Therapy,* ed. Murphy (Boston, 1979), pp. 238–244.

Chapter XXIX

1. This phrase appears to be based on Montesquieu: "Philosophical liberty consists in the exercise of one's will, or at least (if we must speak in a way that will encompass all systems) in the opinion that one has that one is exercising one's will. Political liberty consists of security, or at least of the opinion one has that one is secure." Montesquieu, *De l'esprit des lois* (Caillois ed.), bk. 12, chap. 2, 2:431.

2. In Beccaria's day, judges did indeed exercise an almost unlimited discretion over who would be detained pending trial. Manzoni, *Colonna infame*, pp. 970–972, 983, 991, 1037–1042. See also Randall McGowen, "The Image of Justice and Reform of the Criminal Law in Early Nineteenth-Century England," *Buffalo Law Review* 32:89–124.

3. As a Milanese, Beccaria is, of course, referring to the Lombards.

4. Deportation for penal servitude was common in the eighteenth century. English criminals were frequently transported to the colonies. Closer to Beccaria's home, Lombard prisoners were often sent to serve as galley slaves for the Republic of Venice. Sergio Romagnoli, "Introduzione," *Opere* (Romagnoli ed.), 1:iv.

Chapter XXX

1. Throughout his career, Beccaria continued to insist that the right of private ownership is a social right, not a natural one. See above, Chap. XXII, n. 1. Before Beccaria, Montesquieu had been at special pains to distinguish crimes against persons from those against property. Montesquieu, *De l'esprit des lois* (Caillois ed.), bk. 12, chap. 4, 2:635.

Chapter XXXI

1. Many eighteenth-century legal systems admitted "half-proofs" as evidence; such testimony was usually hearsay. Gay, *Voltaire's Politics*, p. 302; Foucault, *Discipline and Punish*, pp. 37–43.

2. Beccaria's "Newtonian" analysis of sexual attraction may have helped to inspire Bentham's utilitarian ruminations on the subject. Bentham, *Principles* (Burns and Hart ed.), chap. 5, sec. 2, p. 42; chap. 10, sec. 16, p. 104.

3. Montesquieu was notorious for insisting that climate has a decisive influence on sexual desire and that this passion is stronger in warm than in cool countries. Montesquieu, *De l'esprit des lois* (Caillois ed.), bk. 14, chap. 2, 477; bk. 16, 2:508–522, esp. chap. 8, 2:514.

4. Once more Beccaria berates the authority of the head of a household. Beccaria himself had had serious difficulties because his father, Giovanni Beccaria, had objected to his choice of a bride. See above, Chap. XXVI, n. 1.

5. Montesquieu deplored frequent prosecutions for pederasty, pointing out that they opened the door to slander. He also suggested that sodomy would be exceedingly rare were it not for corrupt educational institutions and practices. Montesquieu, *De l'esprit des lois* (Caillois ed.), bk. 12, chap. 6, 2:437–438.

6. Beccaria, like most young men of quality in his day, had been educated in an all-male secondary school; like most of the elite youth of Roman Catholic lands, his instructors had been celibate members of the regular clergy. Beccaria later described his Jesuit education as "fanatical." Beccaria to Morellet, 26 Jan. 1766, in *Opere* (Romagnoli ed.), 2:862.

7. In the eighteenth century, when childbirth was dangerous and abortion a very grave risk indeed, infanticide among unwed mothers was relatively common. Robert Mandrou, *La France au XVIIᵉ et XVIIIᵉ siècles* (Paris, 1967), p. 274; Kaplow, *Names of Kings*, p. 62. In a rather ponderous way, Kant discussed maternal infanticide and came to a conclusion similar to Beccaria's. Kant declared that if all laws and customs make a woman's worth depend upon her sexual purity, and if her bastard is a cause of utter disgrace, then she is in a state of nature with respect to the child. Under such circumstances, infanticide cannot be deemed murder. Kant went on to assert that, since the child entered the commonwealth surreptitiously out of wedlock, it is much like smuggled merchandise, and the law may overlook its destruction, just as it can overlook the destruction of contraband. Kant, *Justice* (Ladd ed.), p. 106.

Chapter XXXII

1. Suicide was usually treated as an infamous crime in the eighteenth century. The "criminal" was often subject to a mock trial, public humiliation, and a shameful funeral. Sometimes all his property, or a portion of it, was confiscated. Maestro, *Origins of Penal Reform*, p. 13.

2. Early in his career, Montesquieu had argued that there was no justification at all for punishing suicide, and, in his more mature years, he had deplored the greed which led rulers to seize the property of anyone who had died by his own hand. Montesquieu, *Lettres persanes* (Caillois ed.), letter 76, 1:246–247; Montesquieu, *De l'esprit des lois*, bk. 29, chap. 9, 2:870–871.

3. In the eighteenth century, most Italian states, including Lombardy, prohibited emigration. Laws to this effect were designed to guarantee an adequate labor supply, but they were almost totally ineffective. Stuart Woolf, *A History of Italy, 1700–1860: The Social Constraints of Political Change* (London, 1979), p. 55. Virtually all of what follows is an attack upon such laws.

4. Pietro Verri had insisted that Lombardy had an unfavorable balance of trade and that every effort should be made to reverse this situation. In 1763 he published a history of Milanese trade and, in 1764, an unauthorized account of the current unfavorable balance. The latter undertaking created considerable difficulties for him. Venturi, *Settecento riformatore*, pp. 690–697.

5. Montesquieu had argued that luxury is necessary in a monarchy because it gives employment to the poor and helps to prevent an excessive concentration of wealth. Montesquieu, *De l'esprit des lois* (Caillois ed.), bk. 7, chap. 4, 2:336.

6. This analysis of the functional relationship of luxury to population, territory, and regime seems to be based ultimately on Montesquieu, but it bears a particularly close resemblance to Rousseau's discussion of the subject. Montesquieu, *De l'esprit des lois,* bk. 7, chaps. 1–7, 2:332–340; bk. 18, chaps, 1–17, 2:531–541. Rousseau, *Du contrat social* (Gagnebin and Raymond ed.), bk. 3, chap. 8, 3:414–420.

7. Pietro Verri, though he was by no means opposed to luxury, hoped for a growth in mass consumption industries which, so he believed, would contribute to greater equality and prosperity. Pietro Verri, "Elementi del commercio," in *Il caffè* (Romagnoli ed.), pp. 28. Beccaria likewise spoke in favor of mass consumption industries in his lectures on political economy. Beccaria *Elementi di economia pubblica,* in *Opere* (Romagnoli ed.), 1:358.

Chapter XXXIII

1. Lombardy, like most European states in the eighteenth century, was divided by internal customs barriers. Indeed, Lombardy did not have internal free trade until 1787. Woolf, *History of Italy,* p. 101. Beccaria, while advocating internal free trade, always tended to think of international trade as a rather exceptional activity. Barriè, in *Storia di Milano,* 12: 443. His remarks in this chapter may well be addressed at least as much to domestic as to international smuggling.

2. Beccaria later wrote a mathematical analysis of smuggling for *Il Caffè;* he sought to describe smuggling by referring to the value of the merchandise, the level of the tariff, and the risk involved. It was a pioneering work in the mathematical treatment of economic issues. Cesare Beccaria, "Tentativo analitico su i contrabbandi," in *Opere* (Romagnoli ed.), 1:164–166, Romagnoli, "Introduzione," p. lxxxii.

Chapter XXXIV

1. Beccaria is referring especially to Facchinei, who indicted *On Crimes and Punishments* on six charges of sedition and twenty-three of impiety. See above, "To the Reader," n. 1.

2. The members of the Academy of Fists generally believed that the laws, customs, and institutions inherited from the past were hostile to economic activity and fatal to Milanese commerce. See esp. Alessandro Verri, "Di Giustiniano e delle sue leggi," and "Alcune riflessioni sulla opinione che il commercio deroghi alla nobilità", in *Il caffè* (Romagnoli ed.), pp. 126–136, 183–195.

Chapter XXXV

1. The right of a criminal to have asylum in churches was ancient and it persisted in some parts of Italy until the middle of the nineteenth century. Such special ecclesiastical privileges were abolished in Lombardy by Joseph II. Maestro, *Cesare Beccaria*, pp. 13, 121.

Chapter XXXVI

1. Feudal jurisprudence was based upon the elevation of private law to the status of public law. In the Middle Ages, betrayal of a person to whom one was bound by feudal ties was considered a terrible crime. For an eighteenth-century commentary, see Hume, *History of England*, vol. 1, chap. 2, pp. 361–363, 386–387.

Chapter XXXVII

1. The use of false and frequently illegal promises of impunity in order to obtain confessions and evidence was a common practice, although many jurists inveighed against it. Such means had been used, for instance, in the 1630 trial of the Milanese accused of spreading the plague. Manzoni, *Colonna infame*, pp. 996–1005.

Chapter XXXVIII

1. Such abuse of language and the propensity to mistake phrases for reality was a favorite target of Helvétius. Helvétius, *De l'esprit* (1759 ed.), disc. 1, chap. 4, pp. 24–32.

Chapter XXXIX

1. In the eighteenth century, most law codes did not distinguish sins from crimes, and states supported official churches, imposing some sanction on those who did not conform. Jenkins, "Varieties of Enlightenment Criminology," pp. 112–117.

2. Montesquieu had argued in magisterial fashion that, once several sects had taken root in a given country, they should all be tolerated. Montesquieu, *De l'esprit des lois* (Caillois ed.), bk. 25, chap. 9, 2:744.

3. Beccaria could scarcely have expected anyone to take this disclaimer seriously. The ideas he advocated gained ground. In 1781, Joseph II established religious toleration throughout the Hapsburg dominions, including Lombardy.

Chapter XL

1. Helvétius had attacked some of these "false ideas of utility" in rather similar terms. Helvétius, *De l'esprit* (1759 ed.), disc. 2, chap. 14, pp. 104–115; chap. 17, pp. 123–130; chap. 23, pp. 165–170; disc. 3, chap. 16, pp. 275–284.

2. Again, these ideas appear to be drawn from Helvétius. Helvétius, *De l'esprit*, disc. 2, chaps. 8–9, pp. 227–243.

3. Such thoroughgoing methodological individualism was quite characteristic of utilitarianism. As Bentham put it, "The interest of the community then is, what?—the sum of the interest of the several members who compose it." Bentham, *Principles* (Burns and Hart ed.), chap. 1, sec. 4, p. 12.

4. These remarks may owe something to Rousseau. When tilting against Hobbes, Rousseau insisted that primitive man was amoral, not immoral, and that he did not gratuitously harm his fellows. Rousseau, *Discours sur l'inégalité*, in *Oeuvres* (Gagnebin and Raymond ed.), 3:152–160.

5. Beccaria's comments on despotism, fear, and the insecurity of a despot appear to be based on Helvétius's development of ideas originally expounded by Montesquieu. Helvétius, *De l'esprit* (1759 ed.), disc. 3, chaps. 18–21, 289–305.

Chapter XLI

1. Such ideas of the purpose of legislation were expounded by Helvétius and by Pietro Verri. Helvétius, *De l'esprit* (1759 ed.), disc. 2, chap. 17, pp. 123–130; chaps. 22–23, pp. 155–165; Pietro Verri, *Discorso sulla felicità* (Emanuelli ed.) pp. 53–60.

2. Montesquieu had argued a similar case, particularly insisting on simplicity, when he wrote of the way in which laws should be framed. Montesquieu, *De l'esprit des lois* (Caillois ed.), bk. 29, chap. 16, 2:877.

3. Beccaria relies on Montesquieu in his account of the depravity and indolence of people subjected to a despotic regime. Montesquieu had held that a warm

climate fosters timidity, cruelty, lust, and despotism. Montesquieu, *De l'esprit des lois*, bk. 5, chaps. 14–16, 2:292–300; bk. 14, 2:474–489; bk. 16, chaps. 1–11, 2:509–417; bk. 17, 2:523–530.

Chapter XLII

1. This statement and much of what follows may be seen as a response to Rousseau's diatribe against the arts and sciences. Jean-Jacques Rousseau, *Discours sur les sciences et les arts*, in *Oeuvres* (Gagnebin and Raymond ed.), 3:3–30.

2. Beccaria himself sought a post in the Austrian administration of Lombardy as early as 1765, sending a copy of *On Crimes and Punishments* with his letter requesting a position. Beccaria to Archduke Ferdinand of Austria, 25 June 1765, in *Opere* (Romagnoli ed.), 2:858–859. He was offered an advisory post at the Russian court and finally became an Austrian appointee in the Lombard government. He remained a civil servant for the rest of his life. Maestro, *Origins of Penal Reform*, pp. 68–74, 110–124.

3. From the mid-1760s onward, the Austrian government employed most of the members of the Academy of Fists—they formed the spearhead of the drive for enlightened reform in Lombardy. Woolf, *History of Italy*, pp. 98–109, 127–128.

Chapter XLIII

1. This entire chapter is directed against the small aristocratic judicial intermediary bodies, notably the Senate of Milan, which acted as custodians of traditional law and prevented effective reform.

Chapter XLV

1. The reference is to *Émile* by Jean-Jacques Rousseau. This educational treatise was placed on the Index in 1763. Facchinei was quick to disapprove of Beccaria's endorsement of Rousseau's educational principles. Facchinei, *Note ed osservazioni*, p. 174.

Chapter XLVI

1. Although he was at odds with Beccaria in some respects, Kant agreed with him on this point, and largely for the same reason: "The right to pardon (*jus aggratiandi*), either by mitigating or by entirely remitting the punishment, is certainly

the most slippery of all the rights of the sovereign. By exercising it he can demonstrate the splendor of his majesty and yet thereby wreak injustice to a high degree. With respect to a crime of one subject against another, he absolutely cannot exercise this right, for in such cases exemption from punishment (*impunitas criminis*) constitutes the greatest injustice toward his subjects." Kant, *Justice* (Ladd ed.), pp. 107–108. Both Beccaria and Kant sought to make justice as impersonal as possible.

Chapter XLVII

1. Hegel fully agreed with Beccaria on this score, arguing that punishments can and should vary according to the degree of a society's refinement or barbarism. "A penal code, then," concluded Hegel, "is primarily the child of its age and the state of civil society at the time." Hegel, *Philosophy of Right* (Knox ed.), p. 140. For a modern view substantially like Beccaria's, see Jan Gorecki, *Capital Punishment: Criminal Law and Social Evolution* (New York, 1983), esp. pp. 31–80.